D1294861

SNIPER

The techniques and equipment of the deadly marksman

SNIPER

Mark Spicer

PUBLISHED BY
SALAMANDER BOOKS LIMITED
LONDON

A SALAMANDER BOOK

Published by Salamander Books Ltd.
8 Blenheim Court
Brewery Road
London N7 9NT
United Kingdom

© Salamander Books Ltd., 2001

A member of the Chrysalis Group plc

ISBN 1 84065 229 2

1 3 5 7 9 8 6 4 2

CREDITS

Project Manager: Ray Bonds
Designer: Mark Holt
Diagrams: Julian Baker
Reproduction: Media Print (UK) Limited
Printed and bound in Spain

THE AUTHOR

Sergeant-Major Mark Spicer has been in the British Army for
18 years, for 15 of them as a sniper. Sniping very quickly
became a passion for him and he sought out and absorbed as
much information on the topic as he could. Following several
operational deployments he was posted to the British Army's
Sniper School as an instructor where he was part of a team
that taught sniping not only to British Army personnel but to
many other nation's militaries as well. His passion and natural
talent for this demanding skill was noticed by the US Marine
Corps who invited him to attend their Advanced Sniper and
Sniper Employment Officers Courses at Quantico where he
attained passes on both courses and subsequently returned to
assist in other Marine Sniper training. He has also worked with
the reconnaissance elements of his parent unit and continues to
be requested by other military units to assist in their sniper
programmes.

AUTHOR'S DEDICATION

This book is dedicated to my father and fellow soldier,
Roy Spicer, whose shoes I always tried to fill and who I sadly
lost four year ago.

AUTHOR'S ACKNOWLEDGMENTS

I would like to thank my wife Carol, son Stephen and daughter
Gemma for their patience and encouragement while this book
was being prepared. I also thank my good friend Harry Furness
for his belief, advice and friendship. In addition, my thanks go to
many fellow snipers for their encouragement in this project, and
in particular to Neil Morris, Nick, Dave Dennis, Daz Williamson,
and Bob Warrener.

CONTENTS

FOREWORD..................................8

❶ THE ROLE OF THE SNIPER.................12

❷ SELECTION AND TRAINING...............20

❸ CAMOUFLAGE AND CONCEALMENT......60

❹ SHOOTING TECHNIQUES....................86

❺ TACTICAL DEPLOYMENT.................112

INDEX.......................................142

THE SNIPER'S CREED

1. You are one of the few remaining warriors on the changing battlefield. You must strive to attain the demands set by your forebears and further those boundaries once they are met.

2. Respect all soldiers and utilise your own knowledge to assist and aid without fostering needless elitism.

3. Be inquisitive and seek out knowledge. You do not stop learning. The sniper has nothing to learn has nothing to live for, and will quickly die.

4. Stay at your peak of both physical and mental fitness at all times.

5. Be courageous without being impulsive, determined without obstinacy and open among closed minds.

6. Never dismiss an idea until it is thoroughly borne out; it may or may not win a war.

7. Never underestimate your enemy, or judge him by previous actions; he may have improved. Out-think your enemy and you will also out-live him.

8. Remain calm and be resolved before committing to action; nobody has less firepower than you.

9. The best rifle in the world is of no use without ammunition; protect your ammunition and use it wisely.

10. Remain true to the simple code of soldiery - first my rifle and then myself.

11. Understand the battle plan fully and how your actions will affect it.

12. Personal integrity and the strength to acknowledge your limitations are qualities not faults.

13. Learn how many defer to rank or status so that in the magnified and silent world of the sniper the leader can never hide.

14. You must protect and save the lives of your comrades by effectively removing danger and not embarking on your own crusades.

15. Initiative, deception and surprise are just as powerful as your rifle; make use of them.

Sergeant-Major Mark Spicer,
British Army Sniper

FOREWORD

BY HARRY M. FURNESS
SNIPER SERGEANT, WORLD WAR II: YORK AND LANCASTER REGIMENT, BRITISH ARMY

Even long after World War II was over, its sniper operations were still widely misunderstood. When a senior figure from within the military, who hadn't served as a frontline soldier, was told that I had served as a sniper, he gave me a rather strange look and said: "Well, I suppose someone had to do it." This didn't come as any surprise to me. In fact, it was a fairly typical reaction I received from many people who had no real knowledge of the tactical and strategic deployment of a comparatively small group of very specialised combat soldiers.

At present the term "politically correct" is bandied about as if it represented a cure-all for all of the problems faced by society. Most politicians wax lyrical on how "correct" they are. But ponder awhile on the truth behind one of Rudyard Kipling's many military verses: "For it's Tommy this, an' Tommy that, an' 'Chuck 'im out, the brute!' / But it's 'Saviour of 'is country' when the guns begin to shoot." It is a simple truth nonetheless that our soldiers must face up to death and

possible mutilation in dealing with the enemies of our country. Then there is no time for long discussions on human values. That comes later. In times of desperate trouble, you will find our combat snipers out there, always ahead of our foremost battle lines, dedicated to carrying out a thankless but very necessary task. This book provides an invaluable insight into the snipers' hazardous role.

The duties of the combat sniper are numerous, and very different to general perception. For example, an expertly trained sniper would never climb a tree to shoot at the enemy. Neither would he ever consider using a high clock tower or church spire as a shooting platform. Those fancy antics are found only in Hollywood movies. A sniper will avoid any kind of position that seems obvious. Yet one still hears those hoary old soldiers' tales of snipers being shot out of trees and towers, though very few, if any at all, have any foundation in fact. However, it must be said that, in the Pacific campaign, Japanese riflemen mistakenly used trees and were promptly dispatched by a burst of automatic fire from the advancing infantry. But they were hardly specialist-trained snipers who use cunning and operate from well-concealed ground level positions. Then again, in almost every war movie, we see soldiers waving helmets on sticks. This is supposed to attract sniper fire, so that the snipers will give away their positions. In real warfare this would be a major and costly error. No real sniper would be fooled by such a silly move. Quite the reverse. It would give him the chance to pinpoint the exact position of possible targets which he would take out when those troops tried to advance.

Since sharpshooters first started to make their presence felt on the battlefield, their skills, techniques and advanced weaponry have made them an invaluable part of every army. Most countries now have well-organised sniping schools, providing advanced training by highly qualified instructors who have seen active-duty service as snipers themselves. The snipers' contribution to frontline strategy has long been recognised, so they are never used as if they were suicide troops. They never take unreasonable and foolhardy chances. Everything they do in their operational role is based upon calculated risk, evaluated from their extensive training and experience. Well-rehearsed camouflage techniques ensure that a sniper will only shoot from the most unexpected places. After only one shot, or at most two, he will withdraw to a pre-determined position from which he already has a well-worked out escape route. In former campaigns it was not unknown for snipers to construct natural-looking "hides" which were used for short periods. But modern-day deployments see the sniper more as a ghostlike figure capable of moving unseen around the battlefield, constantly changing positions to bewilder his enemy.

So how has the sniper's specialised techniques evolved over the years? When we ask this question we immediately need to clarify one thing. At no time does a sniper stick to a rigid set of rules. He avoids anything that might be recognised as a routine. The only rule is that there are no rules. Only that way does he have a chance of deceiving enemies who often have a high degree of expertise themselves.

Admittedly we have all learned through the costly mistakes made by earlier snipers who, through even minor errors of judgement, now lie in shallow graves. Their mistakes are related in our extensive training programmes as a warning. In World War II, it proved to be our good fortune that the Sniping Schools attracted the finest officers and NCOs, many of whom had previously been first class hunters. Today under the mantle of NATO, we also have an excellent exchange programme under which our active-duty snipers have the opportunity of gaining additional worthwhile experience by being attached to the sniping establishments of other friendly countries. Our close links with the American military has undoubtedly advanced the skills of both nation's sniper specialists in what are now considered high-tech sniping operations. World War II sniper missions were mostly confined to the period from just pre-dawn to shortly after dusk in the last available light. The time in between was often spent in reconnaissance so that the sniper could reach unobserved suitable positions. Now sniping continues around the clock, throughout the blackest night. And they take place in near silence with the new sub-sonic sniper rifles.

Combat snipers are always specialists, carefully selected from volunteers who must undergo long and intensive training before they can qualify for assignment to their regiments. Then they will enter a type of service which is known to be the most lonesome and hazardous of any fighting unit. The order of battle for attached snipers is quite different to the typical duties of a line infantryman in a rifle company. Snipers make flank attacks to eliminate "priority targets". Snipers are not expected to take land. Nor do they become involved in taking prisoners. Neither would a sniper ever make a bayonet charge. To defend land taken against attacking enemy infantry is a priority task. But it is in providing a "sniper shield" well forward in no-man's-land that the sniper really comes into his own. It is then that he takes on that most dangerous of tasks – the elimination of enemy snipers. In action, the sniper lives a constant battle of wits in which the most competent and cunning will withdraw, leaving behind his opponent dead.

Too often it is assumed that snipers will shoot at anybody or anything that moves into the vision of his telescopic sight. That is no longer true in most conflicts. Certainly in the early stages of World War I, archive records show that any movement in the trenches attracted sniper fire. But this, in turn, enabled expert observers to pinpoint and deal effectively with those careless enough to give away their positions. Well-trained snipers reserve their fire until they can engage a priority target. They do not fire random shots, nor will they take part in general harassment fire in the hope of keeping enemy heads down. The operational sniper fires his rifle only rarely. He moves often, using his highly developed marksmanship skills with intent. One shot, one kill is his creed. It is this that makes the sniper the most feared soldier on any battlefield.

It appears to be an ongoing theme of the news media to malign upon sniper activities. Reports talk emotively of the cold-blooded killing of women and children, or other innocent civilians who have strayed into the gunman's sights. Undoubtedly many civilians are unfortunate enough to become casualties of war, but it is a common journalistic error to attribute their deaths to snipers. It makes a better story it seems. In fact the real villains are non-specialist and undisciplined soldiers or guerrilla fighters who don't give a damn who they shoot. It cannot be over-emphasised that specialist-trained operational snipers are very selective in their choice of enemy targets. These are stalked and killed with just one shot at almost any distance, even in the most foul weather conditions. Another common fallacy is that snipers would prefer to wound rather than kill outright – the idea being that it ties up manpower and resources to carry a wounded man off the battlefield and care for him afterwards. It is of course utter nonsense. Every sniper school teaches just one thing – the outright instantaneous kill. With a high precision shot from a skilled sniper, the soldier targeted never knows what hit him. He is dead before he hits the ground. This basic fact makes the specialist sniper the most dreaded enemy of all soldiers.

However, killing priority targets is not the only task undertaken by snipers in action. Each sniper also supplies valuable field intelligence when he returns to his regimental lines. During his debriefing, he provides field sketches showing the most forward areas he has scouted, together with pinpoint accurate map references and detailed observation reports of enemy positions. These reports are needed not only by his battalion C.O. but will also be passed back to the intelligence officers at brigade and division level.

Combat snipers operate covertly, often alone or, at most, in a team of two specialists combining the role of sniper and observer. Being detached from the main body of troops leads at times to possible misunderstandings through the lack of shared information. Typically mission details are not considered to be relevant information to be shared among the lower ranks of rifle companies, provided the senior regimental officers are kept advised on planned sniper operations. In practice this leads to a misunderstanding of the sniper's role. In the American campaign in Vietnam, US servicemen used to refer to their scout snipers as "Murder Incorporated". They were just thought of as assassins, and tales of their body-counts increased as each soldier passed on the story. It cannot be overstated that snipers do not murder soldiers. There is a profound difference. They kill using the reason and judgement under internationally agreed rules of war.

But right from the start it needs to be said that a highly specialised book on the subject of military sniping is not for the squeamish. This is a time to call a spade a spade. After all the primary duty of the combat sniper is to kill people, albeit that they are typically the soldiers of an enemy country. I am glad to be given the opportunity to introduce this book written by Sergeant-Major Mark Spicer. He is a widely acknowledged Master Sniper with the British armed forces. Not only does he serve as an active-duty sniper specialist with his infantry regiment, he is frequently seconded to the overseas military establishments within NATO who request his expert services to train their own specialists in high intensity sniper training programmes. In recent years he has also been in demand as a lecturer in the US for both military and law enforcement snipers. Having also served as a senior sniper instructor at the British Army Snipers' Battle School, he provides an excellent guide to the reader who wants to research this hugely complex subject.

It is vital for the reader of these pages to understand that much that appears in the general news media is misguided. Many sensational articles and TV reportage is often as far from the truth as it is possible to get. According to many newspaper and TV reporters, every stray shot fired in any conflict is attributed to sniper fire. Even random artillery fire has been described as sniping by some journalists. Such reporting is unreliable and utter nonsense by any standards.

ABOVE: Sniper Sergeant Harry M. Furness trained as a specialist on sniper courses at Bisley Small Arms School, Hythe School of Musketry, and at The Army School of Sniping in Llanberis. In action as an operational-sniper from Normandy landings, across france, Belgium, Holland and into Germany, 1944/45. Twice walking wounded, and mentioned in despatches for sniping activities.

So who makes the best snipers? This is a question often asked even by soldiers. Certainly it is not the Rambo-type, the hot-headed, or anyone filled with hate. Any one of those conditions would cloud the sniper's judgement. Before volunteering to train as a sniper, the trainee must already be a skilled rifle marksman, capable of high-precision shooting to extreme range, able to cope with the most foul weather and still hit his target. He needs the soul of a hunter, the patience of a saint and have full control of his innermost feelings so that he can complete his macabre missions. The task is far from easy; the dangers exceptional. It is as well to bear in mind that snipers must expect vicious retaliation from an enraged enemy. Bearing in mind these provisos, the role of a sniper would suit those who have confidence in their skills and who do not need the close comradeship of other infantrymen around them in battle. The sniper is a loner, self-motivated and fully dependent upon his own initiative in his dangerous tasks. He has the unique advantage of being his own boss in action. This is rare in soldiering where most men are under constant supervision.

One very important aspect concerning the sniper that never seems to get mentioned is the fact that snipers save lives. Walking around today are very many former officers and NCOs who would have been targeted and killed by enemy snipers if it had not been for what is known as the "sniper shield". This very efficient tactic is in constant operation in war. Dedicated sniper teams operate far beyond a regiment's foremost positions and stalk, counter and eliminate enemy snipers. Those enemy snipers would otherwise cause devastating losses among our best battlefield leaders.

Books on military sniping are few and far between. This is possibly because many feel uneasy when faced with the truth of what war entails. So apart from scarce "restricted issue" official training manual guides, the number of factual books relating to snipers is extremely limited. So this excellent new book coming from Sergeant-Major Mark Spicer is a most welcome addition to the literature, more so because it provides an interesting insight into the covert world of publicity-shy specialist snipers who, at great personal risk, will continue to deploy and defend our best fighting soldiers in conflicts still to come.

THE ROLE OF THE SNIPER

The art of sniping can be traced back over many years, but while the battlefield and the technology deployed on it are constantly changing, the basic art of sniping has not. Certainly, the sniper today has to consider and understand the capabilities of new technologies and how they will affect his deployment, but in essence sniping still consists of one man with his rifle who has the capability to cause mayhem in a much larger force.

Many people have linked modern day snipers with the archers at Agincourt, when England's Henry V defeated the French in 1415. But this is not a true analogy, since although Henry's victory came mainly through the overwhelming superiority of the English longbow, causing more than 6,000 French casualties for the loss of 1,600 Englishmen, the arrows were not in the main precision-targeted projectiles. The first real conflict to which sniping can be traced was the British Army's clash with the colonial forces in the American War of Independence (1775-1783). Here the Americans deployed highly trained marksmen to the flanks of the highly visible and tightly packed British forces, causing havoc and inflicting high levels of casualties. At the time it was considered unfair and without honour, but it was nonetheless very effective and eventually forced a rethink on the part of the British.

Moving on through history we witness the British Army's first real moves into the world of sniping with the formation and deployment of the 95th Rifles (the modern day Royal Green Jackets) and the King's Rifle Corps during the Peninsular War against France (1808-1814). Sir Arthur Wellesley (who became the Duke of Wellington) deployed small groups of soldiers, dressed in dark green uniforms instead of the more traditional red, who used the famous Baker rifles to pour accurate fire into the advancing French troops before they came into range of the musket-armed British battalions. Known as "skirmishers", these troops were the first British soldiers to adopt a camouflage uniform of dark green, and used small groups and manoeuvre tactics to press home their advantage.

Sniping continued to play a significant part in warfare in the coming years. During the American Civil War (1861-1865) a few US units won special notice for their rifle skills, none more so than the 1st and 2nd Regiments of US Sharpshooters, commonly known as Berdan's Sharpshooters after the colonel of the 1st Regiment, Hiram Berdan. Seeing their role as skirmishers and specialist marksmen, Berdan selected experienced men and armed them with the best weapons available, the Sharps .52 calibre rifle. Many also carried telescopic sights. With a view to camouflage, Berdan also clothed his men in green kepis, or hats, and dark green uniform blouses. In keeping with the rest of the army, their trousers were at first light blue, but these too were later changed to green.

LEFT: Major Hesketh-Pritchard, DSO, MC, commander of the first sniper, observation and scouting school for the British Army during World War I.

ABOVE: Captain Herbert McBride. An American, he joined 21st Battalion Canadian Expeditionary Force to enter the fighting during World War I.

The British, again, suffered at the hands of snipers during the Boer War in South Africa (1899-1902). As they were to do many times in the coming years, the British had abandoned all they had learned before, but they finally adopted a more suitable colour of uniform for all soldiers in an attempt to limit the Boers' ability to pick off their troops easily.

Throughout this and previous periods of military history the art of shooting someone at distance and from a concealed position was considered to be cowardly and just not the done thing. Therefore, the skill was never really accepted, while the cavalry and lancers were considered the ultimate weapons of war.

World War I was to change all that and snipers really came into their own. With all both sides bogged down in trench warfare, anything that would give an advantage was considered. The Germans had within their ranks a wealth of marksmen who had been gamekeepers in their large forests. They not only had the natural hunter's instincts, but also a wide selection of optical sights fitted to hunting rifles, and very quickly used them with devastating effect against the British troops in the opposing trenches. Within weeks the term "sniper" became the scare word in the trenches; indeed, the British lost up to a hundred men a day to this "new" threat on some sectors of the front lines.

Appalled at the losses being inflicted upon the British, Major Hesketh-Pritchard, who had been a successful big game hunter before the war, became the driving force behind the British response, and was instrumental in the establishment of the first British Army sniper course. In this course he laid down the fundamentals of what he believed went together to make a good sniper, and in doing so can rightly lay claim to being the "father" of British sniping. Hesketh-Pritchard believed that to succeed as a sniper an individual must have the following qualities: (a) a hunter's instinct; (b) enduring patience; and (c) acute powers of observation.

He also stated that any man could be trained as a deadly shot with a telescopic sight, but that it took true dedication to become a sniper. The Hesketh-Pritchard school very quickly produced some very effective snipers and within a very short time the British had turned the tables on the German forces. Hesketh, or "Hex" as friends knew him, became established as an authority on sniping and was constantly referred to by the army high command as the "king of the snipers". The troops, on the other hand, had a different and less complimentary name for him – "The Professional Assassin". While primarily the commandant and chief instructor of the 1st SOS (School of Sniping), he was continually assisting armies of other nations in establishing their own schools, which steadily increased in number. Hesketh-Pritchard and other influences, such as McBride, Gaythorn-Hardy, Langford-Lloyd, Captain Underhill, Major George Gray and Major Neville Armstrong, all played their part in expanding the acceptance and use of sniping within the British military. The snipers were very quickly found to have another and sometimes more important asset as a result of their training, that of observation.

A very important part of the sniper's training is the ability to notice things on a battlefield that the average soldier would miss or just discount. This attention to detail is essential to the sniper if he is to remain alive, since to discount or fail to notice something out of the ordinary could well lead to his death. Armed with this invaluable skill, the newly

deployed snipers during World War I very quickly started to notice changes in their areas of operation or the enemy's routine, and by committing it all to their log books for passage up the chain of command to the battalion intelligence officers, helped paint a very detailed "larger picture". One such example was when a British sniper noticed that, on a certain part of the German parapet to his front, there was always a very well-fed cat that remained within a tight boundary. This led him to believe that the cat was being well

ABOVE: The two main types of camouflage suits used by British snipers in WWI were the "Simian suit" (left) and the "Boiler suit". These were primarily made of old sacking material and painted in disruptive colours to match the surrounding battlefield. They were over-large, and bore no real shape, the first recorded efforts by British units to break up the prominent outline of a man.

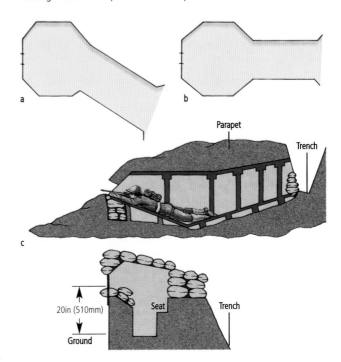

ABOVE: Illustrations of the designs and thinking behind WWI British sniper trench positions. Fig (a) indicates the need to offset the firer's position in relation to his rifle. This not only provided him with a more natural shooting position, but also meant that any incoming fire aimed at his firing port if located would not hit him. Fig (c) shows how the sniper's position was dug under and forward of the main trench position, thereby taking him out of the enemy's area of immediate observation and affording him better observation of the ground to his front.

looked after by the Germans within that area and, since he knew that food was in short supply, he reckoned that the cat had found itself some officers to befriend. This observation was duly passed up the chain where the intelligence officer decided to act upon it and the subsequent artillery barrage was later found to have destroyed the enemy command bunker and all inside.

Such skills would provide all sides with invaluable intelligence during the continuing conflict and snipers became as effective with their eyes as they were with their rifles. The advent of the recognised sniper led to all manner of changes to the way that units operated and also to the introduction of new equipment. Troops in the trenches could never predict where the sniper could see and hence shoot, and this meant that to stick their heads above the parapet was a very risky pastime. As continual observation of the enemy was essential, an alternative was needed. The answer was the development of two main options, firstly the introduction of trench periscopes that enabled the observer to watch the enemy without sticking his head up, and secondly the construction of loophole observation points suitably camouflaged from which to observe unseen. With the second option, while the Germans cleverly hid theirs, the typically British attitude of parade ground neatness soon led to their discovery and engagement by enemy snipers. The answer was to fit the loopholes with steel protective plates, but this simply led to another innovation with the issuing to German snipers of armour-piercing ammunition. The race for supremacy has continued through to today's snipers, and indeed the ability to out-think the opponent is the heart of surviving in this very risky trade.

By the mid point of the war, the British battalions had sections of snipers performing observation and intelligence-gathering roles on all major fronts. Even at this early stage of the sniper's evolution, using a pair of men was found to be the best working solution, with a dedicated firer and an observer. The pair were usually allocated stretches of trench that were their responsibility, and within that area they would have several hides and loopholes from which to work. The snipers would not only shoot any enemy targets that became visible, but also build up a pattern of life and log any activity along their sector for passing up the intelligence chain. This skill and dedication was to provide much valuable information throughout the war.

With the impending arrival of the Americans into the war, and as a result of the US Army requesting the exchange of British sniper experts to teach in the United States, Lieutenant George Gray, one of Hesketh's instructors, was chosen and promoted to major and sent to the US. With him he took a training team of officers and NCOs, all suitably experienced, and proceeded to pass on the valuable lessons already learned in the trenches. The Americans provided an area of land on which was constructed an exact replica of both German and Allied trenches. A copy of no-man's-land was added and examples of both good and bad hide and loophole positions were constructed. After teaching several courses on sniping and scouting to the US 28th Division, the team returned to France, with Major Gray taking command of all snipers within the 38th Division. It can be appreciated that, with this exchange of training, Hesketh's ideas heavily influenced American sniper training, and this training went on to produce some very successful snipers. Among them

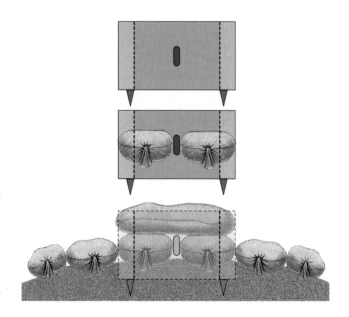

ABOVE: Snipers went to great lengths to conceal themselves from the enemy and hence his fire. This illustration shows how snipers were taught to insert an iron sheet with a firing port cut into it, known as a loophole, into the sandbag revetments of the defending trenches to allow them to observe and engage targets without compromising their location. The German snipers were particularly skilled in this form of camouflage.

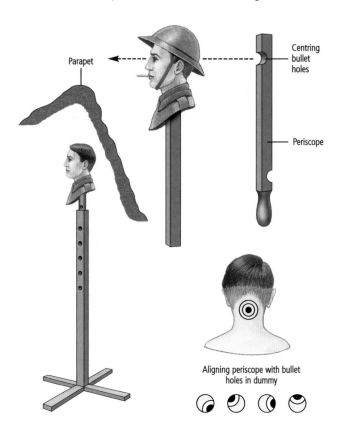

Parapet

Centring bullet holes

Periscope

Aligning periscope with bullet holes in dummy

ABOVE: During World War I, one method employed to locate an enemy sniper was to entice him to shoot at a deception device such as a dummy head of a soldier. A trench periscope could be installed in the dummy (or held in alignment with enemy bullet holes in the dummy head) so that an observer could look back through the dummy along the line of the shot, and hence towards the location of the sniper. This would at least give a general area to observe and could be done without endangering an observer's life.

was a Native American soldier, Private North-West Wind, who went on to be credited with 58 hits before returning to the United States after the war.

The evolution of sniping techniques also led to some very ingenious deceptions and decoys. Hesketh himself had engineers attach flesh-coloured croquet balls to a thin piece of cord at even spacing. These then had general-issue head-wear attached to them and, with snipers already deployed, the whole contraption was marched loudly along a trench to simulate troop movement. When German riflemen appeared to engage these "foolish Tommies", the Allied snipers promptly dispatched them.

With the end of the war came the general assumption among the hierarchy of the armies that the "cowardly" act of sniping at one's enemies without giving him a fair and hon-ourable chance was no longer needed and that snipers should be removed from the order of battle immediately. This trend swept through all armies and protests by the likes of Armstrong and Hesketh Pritchard that they would need those skills again fell on deaf ears. However, the turmoil that World War I left across Europe soon led to the events that started the World War II, and its coming brought about the return of the sniper.

The Germans had not ignored the effect that well-trained marksmen could have on an opposing force, or the fact that sniper units could have results far out of proportion to their size in relation to the enemy. They established professional and well-equipped sniper schools in their rebuilding of the German Army and, by the opening of hostilities, were very well stocked with skilled and motivated snipers. The other armies of Europe soon rediscovered the staggering damage that the German snipers could inflict upon the command and control of their troops, not to mention the effects on morale and discipline. The British quickly re-established their own sniper schools and recalled the men who had warned of the

mistake in ignoring sniping or moved them back into the role of instructor so as to remove the obvious deficit now facing the British Army.

The forsaking of sniping training between the wars had not been confined to the British. During t World War II both the Americans and the Russians found themselves on the receiving end of very costly lessons that resulted in consid-erable loss of life. The Finns, with good knowledge of the terrain and sensible placement of assets, gave the invading Russian Army a very bloody nose in the winter of 1939. This confrontation produced two of the all-time highest scoring snipers in the form of Kolkka and Hayha, who shot 400 and 505 Russians, respectively. This led to the Russians investing quite considerably in the use of snipers over the coming years; while the operating doctrine of the Russians was much more broad in its outlook, the premise was the same – one man, one rifle, maximum devastation.

With the German invasion of the Russian homeland and the near-collapse of the Soviet Army, snipers were very quickly in the forefront of Russian defence. It was in the defence of their main cities that the Russian snipers made themselves most felt. The Russians used their snipers to move among the German invaders and to engage them from both short and long ranges, giving them no quarter or safe areas. The Russians also employed female snipers, some-thing no other army had done, and they very quickly proved that women can just as easily possess the right qualities to be successful snipers as their male counterparts.

The defence of Stalingrad produced one of the most quoted sniper stories of all time, that of the duel between Major Konings and Vassili Zaitsev. That both men existed is beyond doubt, but whether they actually engaged each other in battle is open to question. The story has it that, following the publicised successes of Zaitsev and other Russian snipers who were decimating the *Wehrmacht* in the rubble

Bᴇʟᴏᴡ: A World War II German sniper engages targets in an urban environment, where his very good rural camouflage is unsuitable for the straight-line shapes of his surroundings.

Rɪɢʜᴛ: A museum exhibit in France displays the excellent advances in camouflage uniform the German military were making during World War II. They were a long way ahead of the Allies.

ABOVE: Dr. Roger Paine, one of the UK's main sniper memorabilia collectors, holding a very rare find, a WWII German sniper rifle suppressor.

BELOW: German WWII sniper rifle suppressor, a very simple device that was slipped over the barrel and held in place by a swinging bracket and threaded bolt. It was found in Normandy.

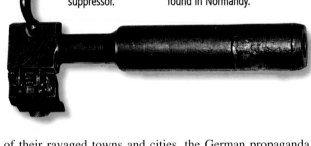

of their ravaged towns and cities, the German propaganda machine decided that the German image could not be seen to be damaged by a mere "Slav" and so sent their top sniper instructor, Konings, to Stalingrad to eliminate the Russian. The fanfared arrival of the German gave Zaitsev prior warning of the coming duel and after several days of stalking each other Konings is said to have made a mistake that led to his death and which also guaranteed the entry of both of them into sniping folklore. Whether true or not, this story demonstrates the dramatic effect that snipers can have on both military planning and the imagination of troops from all sides: if the sniper has any level of success he is credited with almost mystical abilities. Zaitsev went on to kill over 140 German soldiers and was awarded the Order of Lenin.

Throughout the war snipers made their mark in every theatre of operations. The American operations to retake the Pacific Islands were plagued by stay-behind Japanese snipers and sharpshooters, who caused many casualties and held up numerous advances.

In Europe the Allied landings at Normandy were also the targets of German sniper operations, although not to the extent of rumour that had a sniper in every bush and hedgerow. The German snipers were a hindrance to the Allied advance and were found to be using suppressed rifles and ammunition. The deployment of Allied snipers went part way to removing the threat and there are some interesting recorded encounters between them and German snipers.

Amazingly, most of the world's armies once again dropped sniping very soon after the war. Even for those that did not, training of snipers was definitely placed on the back burner with the obvious outcome of a loss of experience and knowledge. The British Army actually discontinued sniper training in the 1950s and would no doubt have lost all knowledge of the skill if it had not been for the Royal Marines who realised the potential of the sniper and kept the

ABOVE: Captain Clifford Shore, R.A.F. Regiment, another pioneer in the field of sniping who during the later stages of the war became one of the British Army Sniper School's instructors.

BELOW: The front cover of the British Army sniper-training manual from WWII. This copy was issued to Harry Furness whose initials can be seen in the stamped panel.

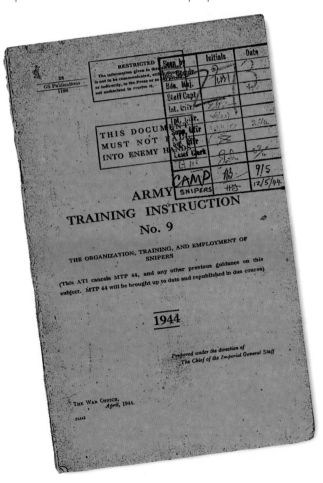

LEFT: The author (left) with successful US Marine Corps Vietnam War sniper Chuck Mawhinney (centre) during a recent sniper event in Phoenix, Arizona.

ABOVE: French Infantry soldier's sweatshirt design from the Balkans conflict demonstrates that UN troops had to overcome early problems with local snipers by deploying their own.

trade alive. As a result of the American and Australian experiences in Vietnam, the British Army once again introduced sniping to the order of battle in 1968 and, thanks to the foresight of the Royal Marines, very quickly made up lost ground.

The conflict in Vietnam provided the Americans, and in particular the US Marine Corps, with some very successful snipers. These men endured some very uncomfortable conditions and were working against an enemy who was not only very efficient, but also was very adept at camouflage and concealment. To have been so successful against this type of enemy is a tribute to men of extreme skill and professionalism, among them Carlos Hathcock and Chuck Mawhinney, whose names have become legend.

Over the following years snipers were to appear in many conflicts, from internal strife through to major armed clashes involving forces from many nations. During the Gulf War of 1991, another US Marine proved the value of snipers by destroying two Soviet-made BMP armoured personnel carriers with two rounds fired from a .50 Barrett rifle. When the Balkans erupted with conflict in Croatia, Bosnia, Serbia and more recently Kosovo, the sniper was again the talk of the world's press, only this time it was not the militarily trained sniper but civilian marksmen using the sniper's skills to cause havoc among the civilian population. While these men and women were not, in most cases, qualified snipers they proved the damage that one person with a sniper rifle can do. The United Nations forces that subsequently deployed to keep the peace all used counter-sniper forces as part of their order of battle. The Russian forces in Chechnya also found out to their cost the threat posed by snipers, and that the only alternative to deploying massive firepower was to insert their own snipers.

The role of the sniper has over the years been confused with that of the sharpshooter, with the likes of police marksmen being labelled snipers when they are not. That is not to say that police marksmen are not very good shots or that they are not every bit as professional as their military counterparts, but that they will never face the risks or have to master the range of skills that a military sniper will in order to survive. For example, the police marksman is not hunted by an armed force in the way that a military sniper is, and does not run the risk of being fired on by tanks, artillery or aircraft if he is compromised. In fact he is very rarely fired on at all if he is seen. Therefore the police marksman will never reach the level of his military counterpart. This is simply because his job does not require him to, and hence he does not train in the same way. Doubtless many police marksmen would reach the standard of the military sniper if needed. Indeed the police have some outstanding rifle shots, but the nature and demands of their roles are different, as summed up in their British Army definitions: "The sniper is a selected soldier who is a trained marksman and observer, who can locate and report on an enemy, however well concealed, who can stalk or lie in wait unseen and kill with one shot. The marksman/sharpshooter is a soldier who consistently achieves a high standard of shooting and who is trained to inflict casualties on opportunity targets using the standard individual weapon."

Whether a military sniper, police or civilian marksman, there is no doubt that the role of one man (or woman) with a powerful rifle is here to stay. The following chapters look at what makes a sniper and how he is used. This book does not cover all aspects of the sniper's world, as one book could never hope to include the wealth of knowledge that has been passed from one sniper to another over the years. What it will do, however, is to dispel some of the myths, particularly about camouflage and concealment, and explain the way that new technology has affected the sniper and his role in today's warfare.

The author realises that one book could never hope to cover the whole world of the sniper as each aspect could be a book in its own right, but hopefully this volume will give the reader an insight into the often mis-quoted or mis-understood role of the sniper. The sniper is not a wild, ill-disciplined rogue warrior burning with desire to kill. He is in fact a very professional, well-motivated and highly disciplined soldier. History can give us countless examples of how an individual has held up, or put to flight, a far superior force with cunning, tactical awareness and precision shooting.

With each technological advance has come the cry "the end of the sniper", and yet still he survives. The reason for this longevity is the sniper's reliance upon the tried and tested methods of combat, which are based on hard work, thought and sweat – not the computer which so many areas of today's military forces depend on. While it is acknowledged that the computer, when working, has greatly enhanced the abilities of a fighting force, it tends to break or fail more times that a man with a rifle, and, after all, no matter how well you can see an area or print out enhanced images of it, until you have a man on it, it is not yours.

The sniper is that man, along with all the other foot soldiers of the infantry who are so often forgotten in today's world that is obsessed with gadgetry and special forces. The special forces soldier is a well trained and highly motivated man, but is more often than not a "jack of all trades and master of none". The sniper is the master of one and, as such, is

a threat to all enemy's special forces. The author has seen on more than one occasion the lowly infantry sniper wipe the floor with his special forces counterpart. This is not to say that special forces men do not make good snipers; it merely confirms that to become a good sniper takes time, and no matter what the name of your unit or however catchy your motto, they will not make you a good sniper. Only time and experience can do that. Unfortunately, too many people think that if you are Green Beret or SAS then you must be the most qualified sniper in the business. The truth is that often the most experienced snipers are to be found in the infantry or marine units where the individuals are not over-worked and under-manned and have the time to dedicate to this most arduous of skills.

Advances in technology will undoubtedly have an influence on the way snipers operate and deploy, but with a dedication on the part of the intelligence services to pass on the operational capabilities of new equipment the sniper can be guided from command levels on how to modify his standard operating procedures (SOPs) and remain effective on future battlefields. The world is changing rapidly with pressure groups and human rights activists having increasing influence on our governments, and hence on the deployment of our military forces. The sniper with his ability to remove a potential or confirmed threat with little or no interference to surrounding civilians is becoming a command asset. The sniper does not cause unnecessary damage to property, he

ABOVE: Author with his partner during the US Marine Advanced Sniper Course, Quantico. US Marine snipers are highly dedicated professionals.

BELOW: The welcome board at the door of the US Marine Scout-Sniper School, Camp Lejeune, indicates the versatility and hard-hitting effects of the sniper.

ABOVE: British sniper pair (left and right) during training in the USA with a US Marine sniper pair. Such cross-training is very instructive for both forces.

BELOW: British Army snipers illustrate the differences between the camouflage and equipment of the World War II sniper (left pair) and that of today.

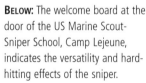

does not kill or injure innocents and he is not exposed to the glare of the world's media since they seldom, if ever, locate his position.

All of this is totally dependent upon the correct time and resources being given over to the selection, training and continuation training of the right men for the job in the first place, and without this armed forces can never realise the potential the sniper offers. This is not to say that the sniper is the answer to all a commander's problems or that the sniper is some form of special forces operative, because he is not. The sniper is very vulnerable and if not supported or deployed in the correct way will very quickly be killed. The sniper can offer the commander an additional asset to support and complement his other assets and, as an integral part of a layered deployment, the sniper can be very effective. The sniper can be found useful employment in all phases of war and on all types of deployment and should be considered by all commanders when carrying out their initial assessments. To overlook the sniper is to waste a valuable addition to the armoury.

The sniper can be used to release much-needed troops from large areas of land that he can dominate from a tactically advantageous position. His ability to act as a "force multiplier" by means of his superior observational skills and his ability to shoot over longer ranges is one that should not go to waste purely because of a lack of understanding or trust on the part of senior commanders.

Armies should endeavour to educate their commanders and ensure correct standards are initiated and maintained within their fighting units. Individual commanders should not be allowed to let sniping standards drop. The tendency now is for commanders to claim that the low pass rate is indicative of a need to lower the standard. This is not so. It is an example of how the instructors are not selecting or are not being allowed to select the right man for the job. High sniper standards worked in all-out war and they will still work today if commanders will allow the correct training environment to be created and not expect every student to pass. Sniping is not for everyone; it takes a special type of individual and identifying these men early on is the key to higher pass rates, not the lowering of standards. Snipers should be pitted against friendly troops whenever possible, in order to hone their skills, and wherever possible they should be deployed on weapon simulation exercises such as the British TESEX where their effect can be registered as to both their knowledge and experience.

Opposing forces soon grow to respect the abilities and dangers of the sniper. The sniper has been on the world's battlefields for many years, and he will be there for many more to come.

ABOVE: Weapons and equipment that would be issued to a British sniper pair today. Included are (left to right) Accuracy International sniper rifle, Global Positioning System (GPS), compass/maps, wind meter, secateurs, binoculars, one of the ghillie suits (which the sniper would have constructed personally), digging tool, grenades, Browning handgun and standard-issue SA80 assault rifle.

BELOW: By contrast, how the World War II British Army sniper pair would have been equipped. Left to right: Lee-Enfield No4T sniper rifle, compass/map, binoculars, scout regiment spotting scope, standard-issue camouflage outfit, sidearm, digging tool, grenades, suppressed Sten gun. While the equipment may be less advanced than today's, little else has changed.

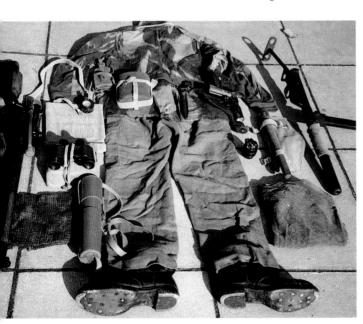

BELOW: On a training exercise, a modern-day British Army sniper pair pause while patrolling to observe and listen for signs of "enemy" activity. Note the variations in their ghillie suits: the man on the right has chosen the German Army fleck tarn camouflage as the basis of his suit.

SELECTION AND TRAINING

The success of a sniper can be traced a back to his selection and training. If the time and effort in identifying the correct type of man for the job is carried out in this early stage, then a unit can expect to have a very useful asset indeed. Too many times men are selected for sniper cadres by officers who do not understand the qualities or the operational requirements of a sniper, so they send men who are almost guaranteed failures, ignoring better suited men who could have gone on to become very successful snipers.

The education and involvement of officers in the selection of snipers is essential in today's budget-related world where armies do not have the cash to waste on training men who stand little chance of passing what is without doubt the hardest field-craft and basic-skills course in the world. The trend among officers is to select the soldiers who look the part or who have drive and aggression. These are not necessarily the right men. The men that should be selected are the ones who are quietly professional and who can go about their business with little or no supervision. The potential sniper is also happy in his own company, yet still capable of relating to the group. He must be a consistently good shot, or at least have that potential, and must be above average in all basic skills, including fitness. He must also have the maturity and sense of humour to cope with life's setbacks.

The list of qualities that commanders should look for when asked to put forward potential sniper candidates varies from one army to the next, and will be influenced by that country's likely areas of conflict, attitudes towards the skill, experiences of sniping, size of the army and mental attrib-

utes of the nation's fitting men. In general a selecting officer should look for the following:

- Above average military skills, paying particular attention to field craft. Either outstanding marksmanship abilities or the potential to be trained. Remember that Hesketh Pritchard said that anyone could be trained to be a good shot with a telescopic-sighted weapon.

- Intelligence is vital for the sniper. Not only does he have to absorb vast amounts of knowledge in training, but he also has to have the common sense to be able to read a tactical situation and assess the consequences of his actions.

- Maturity is also of vital importance to the sniper. He must be aware of his responsibilities and prepared to accept them, have the discipline to work unsupervised and maintain very high standards, while also being a good team player when required. The "lone wolf" is not a good choice as a sniper, as he has to work as part of an overall team and therefore must fit in. And maturity here does not mean age. It means being adult enough to make sensible decisions.

- The fitness of a sniper is another area where corners cannot be cut. The candidate must be of above average

BELOW: British Army snipers and their instructor after successfully completing their sniper course. In the centre of the picture the snipers have used two rifles and a letter board to re-create the image of the British sniper qualification badge.

physical fitness and possess a high level of stamina. The sniper is not a sprinter; he is more of a marathon runner who works slowly but for extended periods. A candidate should not be the man who always runs fastest, rather the man who always finishes with all his kit. The sniper must also possess a good level of mental fitness and not show any tendencies to over-react or become over-emotional in any given situation. Moreover he needs to be in control and display the ability to think things through without losing his temper. And he must be able to accept other people's opinions and criticism.

- A good sense of humour is essential for snipers since their lives are often harsh and unforgiving. Not be able to see the funny side of a situation will lead to stress and mistakes being made. The sniper has to accept that he does not know everything and that he can always learn from others, whether they are more or less experienced than him. The sniper who believes he knows best at all times very quickly dies. Too often snipers and police marksmen take themselves far too seriously. Those who do not believe that there is a place for humour and joking in their training are very, very wrong. The ability of a sniper to joke and to laugh at himself is not just preferable, it is essential. You can laugh at a situation while understanding the seriousness of it; indeed many soldiers use humour to control their fear and to give them the courage to deal with the life-threatening situations they have to face. Humour has its place and should be encouraged not crushed. Just because a sniper may appear to have failed to grasp the seriousness of something, it does not mean that this is the case, but merely that he does not have to maintain an outwardly "hard man" exterior to prove his professionalism.
- The ideal candidate is a non-smoker as the chances of being in an area during operations where it is safe enough to light a cigarette are very slim. As smoking is addictive, a man is more likely to take chances if he feels he just has to have a smoke. Smokers should be actively discouraged, and assistance should be given where possible to help them break the habit.

ABOVE: The author teaching British Army and Royal Marines snipers combat pistol shooting with the Browning pistol. Snipers must be skilled in the use of their sidearm to cover the possibility of close-quarters combat with the enemy if discovered. This is an area that is often over-looked in the training of snipers in other armies.

BELOW: British Army sniper students being tutored in the uses of the pistol in the urban setting. Of particular importance in such environments would be how to reduce their silhouette when engaging the enemy inside buildings. Since live ammunition is used in such training, the simulated building is constructed from wood.

To find men that fit all of these criteria is rare indeed, but if a candidate fits two or more and shows the potential to achieve others he is off to a good start.

So what is a sniper and what is his training trying to achieve? Again, the British Army definition of a sniper is a very good start point when it states: "The sniper is a selected soldier who is a trained marksman and observer, who can locate and report on an enemy, however well concealed, who can stalk or lie in wait unseen and kill with one shot."

The British Army has also laid down seven primary skills that the candidate must possess to become a qualified sniper. These core skills are the building blocks for all other training that the sniper will undertake in his career. Without them he cannot succeed. The seven skills are:

- Shooting.
- Observation.
- Judging distance.
- Navigation.
- Sniper-related knowledge.
- Camouflage and concealment.
- Stalking.

All of these skills are deemed to be essential and to fail to master any one of them is to fail the snipers' course. The reason for this seemingly harsh standard is quite simple. All of the skills combine and complement each other in order to make a successful sniper, who can be deployed under any conditions, knowing that he is trained to a higher standard than his enemy and therefore has a much higher chance of success and survival.

The standards and teaching methods employed on the British Army's basic snipers' courses are very similar to those taught at the first sniper schools in World War I; indeed a sniper from one of those schools would feel quite at home on a modern course. The reason for this is that, although the weaponry and technology has changed beyond all recognition, the role of the sniper has not. The sniper is trained to move and to attack with the minimum of weaponry and assistance, and yet inflict serious physical and mental damage on an enemy. To that end there is no need to change the way the sniper is trained or to change the very high standards set by their forerunners. They had the harsh test of all-out war to define what was and what was not necessary for snipers to survive against overwhelming odds.

ABOVE: Snipers must be proficient in the use of the pistol from any position and from any type of cover. Here they are taught how to engage the enemy from behind low cover. Here, all weapons except the instructor's are cleared and unloaded.

BELOW: Snipers being briefed prior to deployment on training stalk. Note the diversity of ghillie suits and the addition of elastic to allow for attachment of natural foliage. The trousers on the sniper second from left are the WWII issue pattern.

The sniper survives on the basic elements of soldiering that are taught to all infantrymen – those that most forget or are too lazy to use once they finish basic training. With the advances on the battlefield of today, with all its armoured fighting vehicles and precision munitions, some in the military cannot believe that methods first perfected in World War I can still be effective today without modification. In fact, the basic sniper's course is just as effective in producing good snipers today as it ever was. There are, of course, extra skills that the sniper of today must master, but the basic skills to operate and survive as a sniper remain the same.

Although Hesketh Pritchard said that anyone could be trained to be a good shot with a telescopic-sighted rifle, that unfortunately is not always the case. No matter how hard they try there are some soldiers who cannot master ballistics, minutes of angle and correct eye relief. They would be much better suited to a nice belt-fed weapon with a comforting cone of fire. For this reason most sniper courses concentrate on the shooting phase first. If a man cannot master the high standards of shooting required, there is no point in teaching him anything else and wasting limited resources. This may sound harsh, but then so is the enemy. The early removal of a student who cannot make the grade leaves more time and resources to spend on those who can.

The shooting phase of the snipers course is actually the easiest as candidates should have already shown aptitude and be proficient with a service rifle before being selected for the course. All that remains is to educate them on the extra knowledge and flexibility that the sniper needs. The subject of shooting and the various positions and methods used by the sniper is covered in a later chapter. Here we look at the other basic skills needed before a soldier can call himself sniper.

OBSERVATION

The sniper relies on his ability to locate an enemy, no matter how well concealed, so he must have a natural curiosity to investigate and question anything that does not look or feel right. We all have a sixth sense and, in years gone by, would have trusted in it more than we do in the modern urbanised world. A sniper must rediscover that sixth sense. If something does not look or feel right, it must be thoroughly investigated before moving on. To ignore that internal alarm bell can lead to an early grave.

The sniper is trained to not only recognise the unnatural, but to trust in his gut feeling and will investigate any suspicious areas in detail before moving on. The main methods of investigation used are to listen and to look. While listening will pick up any mechanical or human noises present, it is the eye that will locate an enemy in most cases. Locating the enemy by ear will depend upon the quality of troops you are up against. Normal run-of-the-mill soldiers are fairly noisy and lack the self-discipline to control their noise levels. But when you are up against reconnaissance, special forces or other snipers, the chances of locating them through a lack of noise discipline are extremely slim. This is where the sniper's thorough knowledge of camouflage enables him to locate an enemy, however well concealed, with a detailed search of the area, looking for anything that is out of place. The sniper looks for any unnatural patches of foliage, where there maybe a change in direction of growth or a root showing where there should not be one. A colour change may be

BELOW: A British sniper pair during training in the Falklands. Note how the observer is as close to the firer's line of fire as he can get. This allows him to watch for swirl and strike and recommend adjustments to the firer as necessary. It also helps to create an un-human shape and aid concealment.

a give-away and part of a piece of equipment showing, however small, should draw the sniper's attention. The sniper only locates these telltale signs because of the intense observation training he goes through on his basic course. Over the years, he learns that good observation skills and attention to detail are essential to his survival and the methods of training him in this area are very demanding.

The very nature of our life-style has reduced the effectiveness of the human eye, because we just do not normally use our eyes to look over any great distance. The reason for this is that we live and work in urban areas, where our eyes do not have to focus any further than a matter of yards because there always is a building in the way. The eye's muscles, like any other muscle, degenerates if you do not use it and you lose the ability to see things at distance or to notice things in detail. The sniper is trained to both look at areas and objects over great distances and to look at things in detail. And he is trained to combine these skills with the natural curiosity we all possessed as a child, but have lost in adulthood.

The purpose of observation is to locate the enemy. To do that you must be able to penetrate his camouflage. This is achieved with a highly developed sense of sight and a good knowledge of nature. The sniper will depend on his sight to gather intelligence, after locating the enemy, and to ensure his own safety. This means he must not only have a keen sense of sight, but he must also be proficient in the use of any optical aids that may be available to him So the sniper is trained in the correct use and maintenance of binoculars, telescopes and night-vision equipment.

But before a sniper can effectively use these optical aids, he must first master the proper use of his eyes. This is achieved with a combination of physical effort and mental attitude. The physical side of the training takes the form of observing over long distances under operational conditions,

in progressive series of exercises. This training is preceded by mental alertness education, as you can only see something once you are aware that it is out of the ordinary.

The skills used by the hunter in days gone by are a good example for the sniper to follow. The hunter used his powers of deduction to out-guess the animal and to predict what it would do next. Then he would combine alertness and attention to detail to get within striking distance of his target. Alternatively, when he met a dangerous predator, he would use these same skills to avoid becoming the animal's meal, then put himself in an advantageous position. Both these situations that are common when the sniper is out on the battlefield.

The sniper must learn to notice all manner of target indicators or details from which he can make crucial deductions – a wisp of vapour on a cold morning, foliage pointing in a different direction, a sudden and attention-drawing change in colour. All of these would warrant closer scrutiny. When up against a well-trained enemy the chances of locating them through blatant movement or poor drills is unlikely, so it will be the tiny lapses and attention to detail that give them away.

The sudden exit of an animal from an area or the scattering of a flock of birds could indicate the presence of an animal or a human. To ignore it before you assess exactly what the cause of this commotion is could be fatal. Any disturbance of soil should lead the sniper to ask why, and a visual search of the area must then take place in order to find the cause. A discarded food can or wrapper where there should not be one must raise questions in the sniper's mind. Each

BELOW: British Army sniper training in the Falklands. The sniper uses natural foliage and cover to advance unseen onto his intended target. The key to all stalking is adopting natural camouflage and the effective use of dead ground.

ABOVE AND BELOW: Snipers are taught to both observe and avoid any wildlife in their area since each different type will react to human presence in a different way. As an example, sheep happily in a field will bolt away suddenly from any human intrusion. That would draw attention to the area, and indicate to the trained sniper the direction of human presence.

ABOVE: A German Army sniper pair observes the enemy from within a woodline. The observer is using the fallen tree to both cover him and support his optic and thus provide a more stable picture of the area. The sniper is using the "laid-back" firing position.

object tells a story, so there must be a conclusion, and the sniper relies on his ability to notice the absence of the normal and the presence of the abnormal to put him in an advantageous position over his enemy.

The different reactions that animals display when confronted by man can be useful to a sniper, once he is aware of them. For example, sheep will scatter, running in the opposite direction from man's location, while cows, which are naturally curious animals, will move towards the location of man. Cows, which lead one of the world's most boring lives, like to have a good look at something out of the ordinary. If a sniper notices a herd of cows all looking towards the one general area, it would suggest that this area deserves a careful search before moving on. The rabbit is another useful animal. When a rabbit is alerted to a threat it will sit up on its hind quarters and its radar-like ears turn to the direction of the noise or threat, before it bolts away. It is the direction of its ears before it runs away that indicates the direction of the threat, and not the direction it runs in. A rabbit will head for the nearest entry point to its burrow – and safety – and not just in the opposite direction from the threat.

At night, when using night-vision aids, the sniper can use the same early warning methods. Nocturnal animals are just as reliable as their daytime cousins. If you come across deer while scanning an area, it will pay to watch them for a

while. If they hear or smell a threat they will pause and look in the direction of the threat. Then if they turn and run it indicates the threat is approaching. They will run in the opposite direction to approaching threat. The point to remember is that animals often have much better senses than we do and they will detect a threat and react to it more quickly. Also remember that there may be a considerable delay from the reaction of the animal to the arrival of the threat, be it animal or human. Do not allow impatience to get the better of you. If the animal has reacted, the threat to it is real and with experience you will be able to distinguish an animal's reaction to a man from its reaction to another animal. All this is a sorry reflection on man's standing in animal kingdom, but it is a useful tool for a sniper.

The sniper's powers of observation coupled with a good memory make a powerful combination. When a sniper has an area of responsibility he will break that area down into sectors and will then search and scan each, noting all major features and committing them to memory. During his deployment in that area he will re-check each sector many times. If he notices any changes he must investigate them until he can work out why the change has occurred, as it may be due to enemy activity.

The changing light conditions of any normal day can also be of use to a sniper. As the sniper re-checks his areas of

ABOVE: A British sniper aims at his target from within a woodline. Note how prominent the soles of his boots are in comparison to the rest of him. Some snipers make the mistake of overlooking their boots, wrongly thinking that the grass conceals them.

responsibility, the light conditions will change as the position of the sun and any cloud cover alter. The change in light condition brings with it a change in shadow coverage. An area previously covered by shadow may become bathed in light, revealing details formerly hidden and perhaps even revealing a previously unseen enemy. Any large change of light conditions will prompt the sniper to begin a period of renewed observation, even if he has only just finished looking at that area.

Light conditions can also work against the sniper, increasing his fatigue and limiting his vision when the sun is in his face. This also increases the risk of discovery as there is always a chance that light will reflecting off the objective lenses of any optical devise he is using. Covering the lenses with face veil or fitting a shroud to trap any reflected light can drastically reduce this risk. Alternatively you can now purchase lenses covers that are honeycombed to remove the risk altogether, while not impairing the optic's light-gathering capabilities and its performance.

One other point about light conditions that the sniper can use to his advantage is the fact that the air is at its clearest just before and just after rain. This improves light clarity and gives a better depth of vision and detail.

The use of detailed observation and an inquisitive mind are essential in the world of the sniper. A high level of mental alertness and a thorough search process, both physical and mental, is essential. Any object or area of suspicion must be analysed from all angles until it has been identified or removed from the risk category. This is the key to survival for the sniper.

METHODS OF OBSERVATION

To make the most of his observation skills, the sniper must use them in the most efficient manner possible. That requires the use of a system. Whenever the sniper arrives in his chosen position, be it hide or a pause in stalking, he must carry out and immediate search of the area – both close to and further away – to check for threats to his safety. Once he is happy that there is no immediate risk to him, he will then carry out a more detailed search of the surrounding area, and if he is to remain in that location for any period of time he will prepare a range card.

HASTY SEARCH

The hasty search is exactly what the name implies, a swift check of the area for any signs of enemy activity. It should take no longer than thirty seconds. Firstly the sniper will carry out a check of all the prominent areas within his arc, ensuring he works right to left, or left to right, in a systematic manner. This ensures total coverage and prevents him missing any points. While the search is systematic, it is not a sweeping search, but a rapid check of specific points. The reason for this is that, when the eye is focused onto one specific point, the eye's peripheral vision will detect movement over a wide area around that point and alert the sniper to any enemy activity that may represent a threat to his life.

ABOVE: A Gurkha sniper moves cautiously over the brow of a hill, maintaining visual contact with his target at all times. The improvised sight shroud removes the risk of light reflecting off his optic lens, and breaks up the obvious dark circle of the sight.

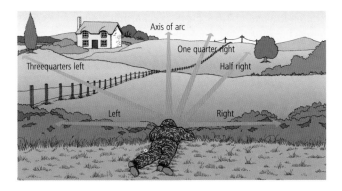

ABOVE: Snipers are taught to break their areas of tactical responsibilities down into sections. This helps them to overcome the problem of indicating a target to a partner or to a nearby supporting sniper pair.

DETAILED SEARCH

With the risk of imminent danger removed by the hasty search, the sniper can now carry out a more detailed search of the area. To do this, the sniper's arc is again broken down systematically and each area is checked in detail before moving on to the next.

The sniper will start at either the far right or far left of his arc and move across to the opposite side, breaking down the ground visually into left, centre and right. Then each sector is searched to a depth of approximately 55 yards (50m). The search will begin with the ground closest to the sniper as this is the area that presents the highest risk to him. Should the enemy make an appearance there, it gives him less time to react. Each sector – left, centre or right – will then be broken down into near, middle and distance. Once the near areas have been checked, the sniper then will move on to the middle ground, being the next area of highest risk. Then the distant will be checked areas to complete the search. At each distance, the left, middle and right must get covered to ensure that the entire arc is scrutinised and each area should be overlapped by about 11 yards (10m) to make sure that no area is missed accidentally.

After the search has been completed, the sniper must keep a check on the area and monitor any areas of interest using the hasty search method. He will also need to carry out a detailed search at irregular intervals to ensure that nothing has changed. If it has, he must use his powers of observation and deduction to find out why. The use of any optical device will, over a fairly short period of time, produce eyestrain or fatigue. This means the sniper will start to miss things and not even realise it, due to reduced effectiveness of the performance of his eyes. If a sniper pair is employed, it is essential that the observation be spread evenly between the sniper and the observer, reducing the chance of missing anything and improving the pair's life expectancy.

OBSERVATION AT NIGHT

The sniper must be just as careful at night as he in the day, and he must not fall into the trap of believing that the darkness will conceal him. The advent of some very effective

BELOW AND RIGHT: During daylight the eye cones, located centrally, are highly effective; by looking directly at your target light falls on the cone cells on the retina and you see the target.

At night the outer rods of the eye are the most effective as they are sensitive to low light conditions; if you look slightly left or right, or above or below your target you will see a much clearer image.

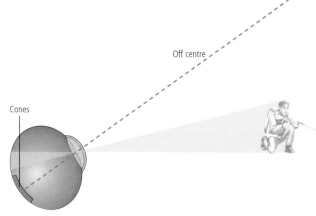

ABOVE: During dark night-time conditions, if the sniper looks directly at his target with the naked eye he will not be able to see it clearly enough to identify or confirm what he is looking at.

ABOVE: If however he uses off-centre vision he will be able to see the target more clearly and hence identify or engage it. This method of observation takes concentration and practice.

ABOVE: While searching at night snipers use the same method as during the day. This involves scanning the area in an imaginary figure of eight pattern, remembering to force themselves to pay attention to the outer area of their vision and not the blurred centre portion which is ineffective at night.

night-vision devices has meant that the sniper – and anyone else on the battlefield – must spend as much time and effort observing at night as he does during daylight. This is obviously harder as the human eye, unlike that of many animals, is not particularly well suited to night vision.

Firstly the sniper must consider the fact that it takes at least thirty minutes for the human eye to adjust to darkness after leaving a lit area, although the wearing of red-lensed goggles can reduce of the adjustment time if they are worn when in lit areas.

The eye uses a different part of the retina at night. In daylight the centre part of the eye is used, while at night the outer part is most effective. For this reason the "off-centre" vision method is employed by snipers at night. This is achieved by looking at about 100 to 150 mils off centre of the object to be viewed. In this way a true image of the objects shape will come into focus. If you try to look directly at an object at night, the image will blur and lose definition due to the inner part of the pupil's lack of clarity in darkness.

NIGHT OBSERVATION AIDS

The most obvious aid for the sniper at night is the abundance of night optics, both passive and active. However each has its limitations and some of them can be monitored by the enemy, betraying your position. In some situations, where you know the enemy does not have this capability, it is possible to deploy IR light sticks, or black light as it is known. In the expected area of enemy activity, in conjunction with night optics, this will illuminate the whole area, unbeknown to the enemy, who believe they are cloaked in darkness.

The option of illumination of the visible or white light type is also available, with the sniper calling for flares or illuminant rounds to be fired by mortars or artillery over an exposed enemy. This tactic is very effective but will cost the sniper his own night vision for the next thirty minutes.

The other option is to use the light gathering capabilities of the normal daylight optics, such as binoculars or telescopic sights. These optics have a quite good capacity to gather available light and allow fairly good identification under low-light conditions. Generally the larger the objective lens, the better the low light performance.

THE RANGE CARD

The sniper, like other soldiers, is taught to prepare either a simple or detailed range card when in a static location for any length of time. This is to aid target indication and speeds up any responses to enemy activity in the sniper's arc of responsibility. If the position is only a short term one, a simple range card will be adequate. Using the card issued the observer will normally fill in the details required while the sniper observes for enemy activity.

Firstly an accurate description of location where the card is being made out is recorded. This allows anyone taking over the position to make use of the information on the card. Next the distance between the marked semi-circles is added to give indication of the range from the position to indicated points on the ground. Then a prominent feature within your arc is selected and marked on the card. A thick line is drawn from the centre position to this point and its range and brief description are marked on the card. This is the "setting ray", and will serve as the marker for all other objects plotted.

The sniper will then decide on a selected number of objects to mark as reference points, such as buildings' gaps in foliage, obstacles or likely enemy approach routes. These are added to the card. To do this, the card is held up to the eye and the setting ray lined up. Then with a pencil the object is marked on the card with its range and brief description added next to it. The trick is to include enough information to be of assistance, but not overcrowd the card and make it difficult or time-consuming to read.

If the sniper is at a long-term position, such as a hide or defensive location, a detailed range card is used. Again a pro forma card issued usually issued, depending upon the army, and it is filled put in much the same way. The main difference with the detailed range card comes with the plotting of the objects to be used as reference points. This time the bearing to the setting ray and to the object is taken and the difference is calculated. Then using a protractor the correct angle from the centre point and the object can be accurately represented on the range card. Again the range and a brief description of what to look for are included on the card.

BELOW: A Ghurkha sniper prepares his range card from his chosen position of observation. The card can be used to record intelligence on the enemy and to also speed up reaction time when indicating areas to another sniper or supporting force via the radio.

ADDITIONAL INFORMATION FOR RANGE CARDS

1. Dead ground.
2. Obstacles, man-made or natural.

3. Friendly force locations, including range.
4. DF (direct fire) tasks for artillery, mortars or heavy machine guns.

TARGET LISTING

When snipers are working from a hide, the enemy is often observed for some time without a shot being fired. This may be because the sniper's rules of engagement do not allow him to engage the enemy, or because he is waiting for a pre-determined H hour. Whatever the reason, it will be necessary to list the targets he locates in to some order of priority, so that when he is allowed to fire he eliminates the most important targets first. If time allows, the targets can be added to the range card with their predetermined ranges and descriptions. This allows for rapid engagement when the time comes. The criteria for the selection of targets is covered in a later chapter, but in essence it is the man or piece of equipment that, if lost, will do the enemy the most harm. Another factor is the distance to the target. As a rule anything over 660 yards (600m) would only be engaged if its destruction is the highest priority. The choice between hitting a man or equipment is take by assessing which would be the most damaging shot.

In some cases, the sniper has to chose whether to fire or to wait and report later, such as not engaging the lead vehicle when it comes into view, but waiting to see the formation and variety of vehicle types in order to identify the type of unit. All of these will have an influence on the sniper's choices when placing targets into order of priority.

SNIPER DIALOGUE

A sniper pair will always keep any verbal communication between them to the bare minimum, to avoid compromising their presence. When it is necessary, a set terminology is used that will keep speech to a minimum. Usually the pair

will have a need to speak when a target has to be indicated and engaged. Each army usually has its own method of doing this. In the British Army a system of pneumonics is used – a pneumonic is a word made up of the first letter of each word in the phrase to be remembered. For example, infantry fire control orders used the pneumonic GRIT which stands for Group, Range, Indication and Type of fire. Snipers use the word EDICT, which stands for Elevation, Deflection, Indication, Confirmation and Time to fire. This would be used as follows:

• Elevation–	[observer]	**629 yards (575m)**
• Deflection–	[observer]	**wind 5 clicks left**
• Indication–	[observer]	**base right corner of red roof house-enemy**
• Confirmation–	[sniper]	**seen**
• Time to fire–	[observer]	**fire**

If at any stage after the observer has said fire and before the sniper releases the shot, the observer notices a change in the wind conditions or notices enemy activity that would endanger the pair if they were to shoot, then he will say "stop". This tells the sniper that there is a problem and he knows not to fire. Once any corrections are made or the threat has receded, the process will start all over again.

USE AND CARE OF OPTICS

The advantage of optical aids when observing are enormous. But if not used correctly or maintained their benefits are soon lost, and under certain conditions when incorrectly used they will give the sniper's position away. Binoculars

BELOW AND RIGHT: The sniper has a constant problem of range estimation from him to his intended target. One answer to this dilemma is the Leica series of laser range finders. These magnificent binoculars are, in the author's opinion, the best option on the market for the sniper and a must if finances permit. The sniper merely aims the binoculars' pointer at his target and presses a button and the range and bearing to the target are illuminated in the sniper's view, giving quick and accurate results when needed on such fast moving targets as helicopters and armour.

BELOW: A British sniper instructor observes for snipers during a training stalk. The snipers must get to within a given distance of the instructor and fire a shot without being located. If a sniper is seen the instructor will guide another instructor onto him.

are the main optical aid of all snipers. They come in many shapes and sizes, from the basic black metal pair to the green rubber armoured Leica Vecta binoculars with built-in laser range finder. Snipers sometimes get to choose their own binoculars; otherwise their government buys them. In either case, they need to be strong enough to do the job and small enough to be carried comfortably while stalking. There is no point in having the world's most amazing binoculars if it takes two of you to carry them.

All military binoculars will have some form of reticule pattern in the lens to aid in judging distance and target indication. It stands to reason that the pattern in the sniper's telescopic sight and the observer's binoculars and spotting scope should be identical. Unfortunately, this is a point that the British Army, as yet, has failed to grasp.

It is best to carry your binocular around the neck as this protects the lens and minimises the movement required when they are needed. To maintain the effectiveness of the lenses, they should not be touched with anything except the correct cleaning materials, such as cleaning tissues or cloth,

to avoid damage to the soft lens glass. On older lenses there may be dark spots or stains. These can be removed by applying a drop of methylated spirits to the lens and gently rubbing it with a lens-cleaning cloth or tissue.

A lot of today's binoculars are self-focusing, but the individually focused type are still available. Everybody's eyes are different and the focus for each eye will vary – even between the two eyes on one person – so the individual focus type should be the sniper's first choice.

It is essential that the focusing procedure is carried out correctly to get the best from the binoculars. Binoculars are hinged centrally so that they can be used by different people with different sized heads and thus different distances between their eyes. This adjustment should be made first before any attempt is made to focus the lenses. The user should start by looking through the binoculars with both eyes open and, using one hand, cover one of the lenses. The unobstructed lens should then be adjusted until the view is clear and crisp. Then the process should be repeated with the other lens. Once this is done, the snipers should note the readings on the lens eyepiece scales so he can quickly reset them in future. On point to note here is to not take too long when focusing. Eyes compensate very quickly and, if a long time is taken, the user will not get a true focus from the optic.

A common mistake when using binoculars is to hold them wrongly, which can reduce their effectiveness. Ensure that the eyepieces are pressed firmly up against the eyes. This reduces the amount of light seeping into the binoculars from the rear, reducing the clarity of the image. Also the

sniper should hold the ends of the binoculars with both hands so that they act as shrouds. This reduces the likelihood of reflected light from the objective lens betraying the sniper's position.

A telescope should be treated in the same way. Remember that the lenses need to be treated with respect. To badly treat optics is to reduce the sniper's ability to observe, and that reduces his effectiveness.

OBSERVATION TRAINING METHODS

When training a sniper to observe, the first thing to do is to improve his memory. As we have already seen, the eye works in conjunction with the memory when trying to identify an object. One way of improving his memory is to run a series of tests that will force the trainee to remember factual and visual items. The tests could start with a series of nine objects placed on a grid so that each object's position can be identified by its grid reference. For example, on a grid with the letters A to F running down the sides and the numbers 1 to 6, a watch may be placed on the grid square A5, a dog tag on D3, and so on. This should be shown to the sniper students for one minute, then covered up. The students should then be distracted by physical exercise to sim-

BELOW: British snipers receiving an important map reading and aerial photography lesson during a basic sniper course. The sniper students are expected to be able to locate several different given targets on the ground and relate them to both the map and the photograph with pinpoint accuracy.

ulate battlefield conditions. After around ten minutes distraction, the students are then asked a series of questions about the objects they saw and their positions, and have to write down the answers. The pass mark is for a would-be sniper 70 per cent; anything below that is a fail.

During these memory tests there should be no communication between the students. While the snipers are usually deployed operationally in pairs, except in special circumstances, training must be conducted individually as both men must be qualified snipers. Only after they have passed the basic course are they taught pair's deployment skills, as a part of their continuation training. Some trainers train snipers as pairs from the outset. This is a mistake. They must be trained to deploy individually to handle the "worst case scenario".

These simple memory tested can be used to improve the sniper student's memory by being made progressively harder. Memory tests should also make use of videos of enemy equipment and radio traffic as these simulate real battlefield tasks.

The next stage is the observation stand. For this the students are shown around twenty different military objects that will be used for all the tests on their course. They will be encouraged to handle the objects and to view them from all angles. These objects form the pool of kit. Every day the instructors will select twelve objects and conceal at ranges from 11 yards (10m) out to 330 yards (300m) within a 500 mils arc. The students will not know which objects have been chosen and, using binoculars and spotting scopes, will have thirty minutes to locate the objects from a static observation line. The objects will have been placed so that they are invisible to the naked eye, but visible with binoculars and identifiable using the powerful spotting scopes. The stu-

ABOVE: French snipers on an observation exercise, identifying equipment placed out by the instructor and plotting them on a panoramic sketch he has drawn.

BELOW: A British sniper observes the enemy with poorly camouflaged binoculars. Note how prominent the circular lenses are against his surroundings.

dents are given ten minutes to draw a panoramic sketch of the arc being observed and all the objects located must be accurately marked on the sketch. Again this is an individual test. No communication between students is allowed and, again, the 70 per cent pass mark applies.

The objects will be placed out in such a way as to show only a tiny portion of its body at an unfamiliar angle. And they will be placed in operational settings wherever possible. For example, a weapon will be concealed with only part of the barrel protruding from cover as it would in real life, and the snipers will be expected to locate it and identify the weapon type by name or country of origin. The reason for this test is to teach the snipers attention to detail and to search and scan correctly. It is this level of expertise that makes the sniper is so deadly on the battlefield.

The objects that are used are very carefully selected to teach the sniper different things about observation. We have already pointed out that nature does not have too many straight lines. This is one of the reasons that things which display a man-made quality in a natural setting are easy to spot. Snipers train picking out objects with these unnatural qualities:

- Glass, as used in optical equipment.
- Metals, with surfaces that shine.
- Weapons, of all types, from all nations.
- Boxes – weapon magazines, food containers and the like.
- Manmade materials – webbing, clothing, ammunition bandoliers etc.
- Straight edges – radio antennas, bayonets, digging tools.
- Cylindrical objects, such as anti-tank missile launchers.
- Colours, such black which is rare in natural settings, or natural colours in odd settings.
- Cord, such as rope, issue string, radio coax.

Only when snipers have mastered these observation skills can their training progress. Some instructors try to

ABOVE: Sniping from a tree is NOT recommended. The tree gives the sniper cover for his shot, but he then has to withdraw, and the trunk offers him no cover. The enemy would be alerted and open fire.

BELOW: A Slovenian sniper in a very effective ghillie suit but who is let down by the prominent dark circles caused by the binoculars' lenses, a problem easily avoided by the camouflage netting over the ends.

push the student too far too fast, arguing that these sort of training is not realistic and does not match battlefield conditions. It is not designed to. It is only when an individual can reach and maintain a high standard required to out live his enemy that the training becomes realistic. This can take the form of a mobile observation stand, where the sniper patrols a designated area, or "lane", with a number items of kit concealed along his route. On completion of the lane he will be expected to answer questions on the lane and the equipment he has passed.

ABOVE: This British sniper pair in training have forgotten a basic lesson. When in the prone position, the soles of their boots are at the same level as their heads, and so need to be camouflaged. Not only are they prominently black, but these also have a very visible manufacturer's label to add insult to injury!

Alternatively, he may be on an observation line watching an arc when an event occurs – such as an enemy patrol moving across his arc, or a vehicle entering it, or a series of incidents that he will be expected to log down or report over the radio. These types of observation stands are progressive, the only limit being the imagination of the instructor. The key to all observation training is to make it progressive and snipers should not be move forward until they can maintain the basic level with consistency.

This observation training for a sniper is very hard and many fail. There is no other soldier, even special forces, who trains to this level of observation. But the reason is that the sniper must see without being seen and kill without being killed.

JUDGING DISTANCE

Another area of military training that is taught to all infantry, yet seldom practised, is that of judging distance. On today's battlefield there is an abundance of range finding equipment from tank-mounted lasers to hand-held lasers to do this job. Indeed snipers are more than adequately equipped in this area. But what happens if the battery goes flat at that vital moment or the forces of Mother Nature con-

spire to break the device? The sniper is aware of these problems though, and in his basic training he is taught several different methods of judging distance without the aid of expensive lasers.

Within military thinking, there are only two main methods of judging distance. They are:

• The appearance method.
• The unit of measure.

Both of these methods are taught to all basic military recruits and, while in training, practised but, due to under-manning and over-deployment there is little time to maintain these skills. For the sniper though, attention to the basic skills is fundamental to success. All the seven sniper skills are constantly practised.

THE APPEARANCE METHOD

This method of judging distance depends upon the memory's ability to retain an image. The way it works is to have a soldier in all his fighting equipment and stand him 110 yards (100m) away from the troops to be trained. The troops then observe the soldier with the eye and any optics available to them as a part of their normal operational kit. They then make a mental note of exactly how much detail they can see on the soldier at that distance. For example, how much of his equipment can be seen in detail? Is his skin tone visible? And are all his limbs and extremities easily picked out?

ABOVE: Ghurkha snipers on an observation training lesson drawing a panoramic sketch of the test area. As a part of the lesson they will be expected to estimate the range to several different points and accurately plot them on their sketch.

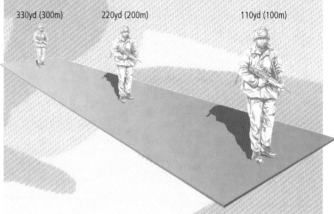

APPEARANCE METHOD GUIDE

- 220 yards (200m) – clear in all detail, colour, skin tone, equipment.
- 330 yards (300m) – clear body outline, face colour good, face detail blurred.
- 440 yards (400m) – clear body outline, all other detail blurred.
- 550 yards (500m) – body begins to taper with head less distinctive.
- 660 yards (600m) – body appears wedge shaped, no head apparent.

Once this is done the soldier is moved back to 220 yards (200m) and the process is repeated. This will continue out to 660 yards (600m) where the detail that could previously be seen is now lost and only the general outline of the soldier can be seen. This method relies on the appearance of a soldier to the eye over a given range and can be effective. But as with all such skills it needs to be practised to remain reliable. Soldiers can also to create an *aide-mémoir* of the detail that can be seen at each given range as a reference for later use. Remember that as each man's eyesight will vary, it is essential for every man to practise and create an *aide-mémoir* individually. For ease of training and to allow for good visual comparison, the instructor should arrange a demonstration with soldiers at all distances. Show each one in turn and describe the points to note. After all have been seen, stand them all up together to allow for a good comparison. It is also advisable to repeat, or include in, the demo, different types of surroundings and varying light conditions to show how these may affect the level of clarity.

UNIT OF MEASURE

The united of measure method of judging distance relies upon the sniper imagining a known distance and comparing it to the distance between him and the target. For example, in the UK the distance that everyone knows is that of a football pitch which is approximately 110 yards (100m). The sniper will visualise how many football pitches will fit into the distance to be judged. So if he imagines that four football pitches will fit between him and the target, it is about 440 yards (400m) away. This system, as with others, requires practice and has two limitations:

- It only works up to around 440 yards (400m).
- It is not effective over dead ground.

When judging distance it is important to know that objects will seem closer or further away under certain conditions. If the soldier is unaware of these conditions or ignores them the range estimation will invariably be wrong.

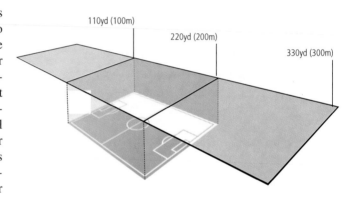

ABOVE: During training on using the Unit of Measure method of range estimation the sniper is shown how to imagine a known distance, such as a football pitch that is about 330ft (100m) long, and then estimate how many football pitches there are between him and the target. For example, three pitches equates to 985ft (300m) between him and the target.

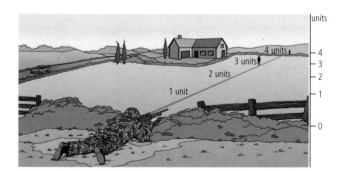

ABOVE: The sniper must learn what familiar objects look like at different ranges, and to judge distances with accuracy. Such objects may well seem further away when the sun is in his eyes; when he is looking down a street or over a valley; when the objects are smaller than their surroundings; and when he is lying down. They may seem closer in bright sunshine; if they are bigger than their surroundings; if they are higher than him; and if there is dead ground between him and them.

FACTORS MAKING OBJECTS SEEM CLOSER

- The object is larger than its surroundings, for example, an armoured vehicle.
- There is dead ground between the object and the observer.
- The object is higher than the observer who has to look up at it.
- Light shining on to the near side of the object, making the detail clearer.

FACTORS MAKING OBJECTS SEEM FURTHER AWAY

- The object is smaller than its surroundings.
- The sunlight is bright or dazzles the observer.
- When the observer is looking down, for example, down a sloping street or a forest track.
- When the observer is lying down.

METHODS OF IMPROVING DISTANCE ESTIMATION

The sniper is trained to cope with the worst case scenario. This means that, no matter what shortage of equipment there is or however bad the situation, the sniper can achieve his mission because he is trained to operate without the reliance on fancy gadgets or technology. That is not to say that the sniper should not use whatever technological aids are available to him, but that he must train without such aids to avoid dependence on them. Having said this, there are several aids available to the sniper when the estimating range to a target and all of them should be used if they available. The sniper must be proficient in the use of all of them to ensure he has the maximum advantage over an enemy. But there are other, simpler methods, of improving straightforward estimates.

KEY RANGES

This method utilises a known range that is then used in comparison to the range to be estimated. In a defensive situation, the range card is an obvious asset when using this method, as it will have known distances pre-recorded on it for objects within the snipers area of tactical responsibility.

SQUAD AVERAGE

This method requires more than one man and the fact that snipers usually work in pairs means that it is a viable option. The two men's range estimates are added together and divided by two to provide an average range to the target.

HALVING

This simple method requires the sniper to estimate the distance to the midway point between him and the target, which should prove easier than estimating the full distance. Then this estimation is doubled giving an estimate of the full distance. The main drawback of this system is that, if the halfway estimate is wildly wrong, the error in the full estimate is doubled.

BRACKETING

With this method the sniper will estimate the furthest range it could be to the target and the shortest range it could be, then work out the mid-point. So if the target is no further than 1,320 yards (1,200m) and no closer than 880 yards (800m), and so the range estimation will be 1,100 yards (1,000m).

ABOVE: A British sniper uses an improvised tripod to give him a stable view of his target through his binoculars. This is essential when measuring the target with the binoculars' reticule in order to assist in range estimation.

RANGING FIRE

This method is not normally associated with snipers' "one shot, one kill" ethos, but when in a defensive position the weapon rules of engagement may allow for ranging fire to take place. In this scenario the sniper should make full use of this option.

BINOCULARS

One of the most reliable and often used methods of range estimation for the sniper is the use of binoculars and a reticule pattern in it. The reticule can be used to accurately measure the target, as long as the object's height is known. The reticule is in mils and 1 mil subtends to 1 yards at 1,000 yards (or 1m at 1,000m), and so the range can be estimated with a fair degree of accuracy. This method is effective over dead ground or when there are variations in height between the target and the sniper. But the height of the target needs to be measured accurately – an accuracy of 0.25 mils is recommended, however too high an estimate will produce better results than one too low. And the optic needs to be resting on a stable base, if not mounted on a tripod. Once the

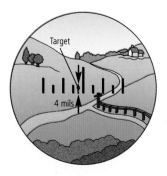

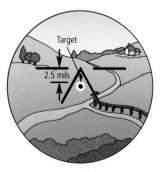

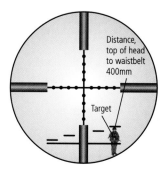

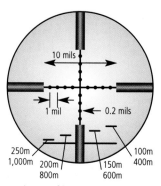

ABOVE: The current reticule or graticule pattern found in British Army binoculars allows the sniper to use the "known height" equation (see below) to estimate the range from the sniper to his intended target.

ABOVE: This pattern is the type used in night sights. Provided that the sniper knows the sizes of each part of the pattern, he can measure his target just as effectively at night as he can in daylight.

ABOVE: These range-finding telescopic sight (left) and telescopic sight reticule (right) designs are found in many of today's sniper scopes. They have built-in range estimation stadia in the lower section of the lens.

Each pair of lines equates to a given range dependent upon whether the sniper measures his target from the waist up, or head to toe, offering a very quick and effective system for engaging fleeting targets of opportunity.

object has been measured the figure is applied into a mathematical equation to give the range to the target:

$$\frac{\text{Known height of target in yards (or metres)} \times 1,000}{\text{Reticule measurement in mils}} = \text{Range in yards (or metres)}$$

For example,

$$\frac{2.5 \times 1,000}{4} = 625 \text{ yards}$$

This method can be used with any optic that has a reticule pattern that is in mils, be it the sniper's telescopic sight, where the current trend is the Mil-Dot reticule, or a spotting scope. The ideal is for the sniper and the observer to have optics that use the same pattern. This will speed up indications and estimations as the pair are viewing the same image

and can converse without moving their gaze from the target. This system will work just as effectively when using metres in place of yards as British forces do or if you use the width of the target instead of the height.

Another method that has been born of this system is that of having prepared charts working on a graph system covering known heights compared to mil sizes. This allows quick reference once the object or target has been selected and measured. It is always advisable to confirm an estimate with a second method if time allows as this will show up an error if the two are grossly different. Many snipers now

BELOW: A British Army sniper using a small calculator to quickly work out the range to a target he has just measured with his optics during a training lesson. The sniper has used a home-made support for the optic to allow for accurate measurement before using the equation to reach an answer.

TABLE OF MILS

SNIPER RANGE ESTIMATION TABLE

Mils \ FT →	2	3	4	5	6	7	8	9	10	11	12	13	14	15	16	17	18	19	20
MT →	.60	.92	1.23	1.54	1.85	2.15	2.46	2.77	3.08	3.38	3.69	4.00	4.31	4.62	4.92	5.23	5.54	5.85	6.15
1.00	600	920	1230	1540	1850	2150	2460	2770	3080	3380	3690	4000	4310	4620	4920	5230	5540	5850	6150
1.50	400	613	820	1027	1233	1433	1640	1847	2053	2253	2460	2667	2873	3080	3280	3487	3693	3900	4100
2.00	300	460	615	770	925	1075	1230	1385	1540	1690	1845	2000	2155	2310	2460	2615	2770	2925	3075
2.50	240	368	492	616	740	860	984	1108	1232	1352	1476	1600	1724	1848	1968	2092	2216	2340	2460
3.00	200	307	410	513	617	717	820	923	1027	1127	1230	1333	1437	1540	1640	1743	1847	1950	2050
4.00	150	230	308	385	463	538	615	693	770	845	923	1000	1078	1155	1230	1308	1385	1463	1538
4.50	133	204	273	342	411	478	547	616	684	751	820	889	958	1027	1093	1162	1231	1300	1367
5.00	120	184	246	308	370	430	492	554	616	676	738	800	862	924	984	1046	1108	1170	1230
5.50	109	167	224	280	336	391	447	504	560	615	671	727	784	840	895	951	1007	1064	1118
6.00	100	153	205	257	308	358	410	462	513	563	615	667	718	770	820	872	923	975	1025
6.50	92	142	189	237	285	331	378	426	474	520	568	615	663	711	757	805	852	900	946
7.00	86	131	176	220	264	307	351	396	440	483	527	571	616	660	703	747	791	836	879
7.50	80	123	164	205	247	287	328	369	411	451	492	533	575	616	656	697	739	780	820
8.00	75	115	154	193	231	269	308	346	385	423	461	500	539	578	615	654	693	731	769
8.50	71	108	145	181	218	253	289	326	362	398	434	471	507	544	579	615	652	688	724
9.00	67	102	137	171	206	239	273	308	342	376	410	444	479	513	547	581	616	650	683
9.50	63	97	129	162	195	226	259	292	324	356	388	421	454	486	518	551	583	616	647
10.00	60	92	123	154	185	215	246	277	308	338	369	400	431	462	492	523	554	585	615
10.50	57	88	117	147	176	205	234	264	293	322	351	381	410	440	469	498	528	557	586
11.00	55	84	112	140	168	195	224	252	280	307	335	364	392	420	447	475	504	532	559
11.50	52	80	107	134	161	187	214	241	268	294	321	348	375	402	428	455	482	509	535
12.00	50	77	103	128	154	179	205	231	257	282	308	333	359	385	410	436	462	488	513
12.50	48	74	98	123	148	172	197	222	246	270	295	320	345	370	394	418	443	468	492
13.00	46	71	95	118	142	165	189	213	237	260	284	308	332	355	378	402	426	450	473
13.50	44	68	91	114	137	159	182	205	228	250	273	296	319	342	364	387	410	433	456
14.00	43	66	88	110	132	154	176	198	220	241	264	286	308	330	351	374	396	418	439
14.50	41	63	85	106	128	148	170	191	212	233	254	276	297	319	339	361	382	403	424
15.00	40	61	82	103	123	143	164	185	205	225	246	267	287	308	328	349	369	390	410
15.50	39	59	79	99	119	139	159	179	199	218	238	258	278	298	317	337	357	377	397
16.00	38	58	77	96	116	134	154	173	193	211	231	250	269	289	308	327	346	366	384
16.50	36	56	75	93	112	130	149	168	187	205	224	242	261	280	298	317	336	355	373
17.00	35	54	72	91	109	126	145	163	181	199	217	235	254	272	289	308	326	344	362
17.50	34	53	70	88	106	123	141	158	176	193	211	229	246	264	281	299	317	334	351
18.00	33	51	68	86	103	119	137	154	171	188	205	222	239	257	273	291	308	325	342
18.50	32	50	66	83	100	116	133	150	166	183	199	216	233	250	266	283	299	316	332
19.00	32	48	65	81	97	113	129	146	162	178	194	211	227	243	259	275	292	308	324
19.50	31	47	63	79	95	110	126	142	158	173	189	205	221	237	252	268	284	300	315
20.00	30	46	62	77	93	108	123	139	154	169	185	200	216	231	246	262	277	293	308

To Use:
1. Estimate height of target and locate across the top.
2. Measure height of the object in mils and locate down the side.
3. Join top and side figs for range to the target.

FORMULA

$$\frac{\text{Height of target (metres)} \times 1{,}000}{\text{Height of tgt (mils)}} = \text{Range (metres)}$$

ABOVE: Most armies today issue their snipers with pre-prepared graphs of height and Mils data. This allows the sniper to measure the target with his optic and, if the target's actual height is already known, he can quickly cross reference it with the graph and reach a range-to-target figure.

carry a small basic calculator, suitably waterproofed and camouflaged, as a part of their personal kit to aid them in their calculations. Even if he is a budding Einstein, a tired man can easily make mistakes – and a sniper should never take risks, only calculated chances.

A method that is also used by snipers is that of measuring the target with the elevation drum of the telescopic sight. For this method the sniper places the aiming point of the sight on to the top of the target and then turn the elevation drum, adding clicks (MOA – minutes of angle) until the aiming point is at waist level on the target. This is then compared to a prepared chart the sniper will have made – he will have measured a man at various ranges using this method and so be able to predict the range.

LASER RANGE FINDER

The obvious choice is to use any available laser for distance estimation. There are certainly some very good options on the market. The Leica series of laser/binocular combinations

ABOVE: A French sniper uses an issued laser range finder to do just that. Users of lasers must be aware, however, that the projected beam can, from certain angles, be seen with night optics, and so can be an indication to the sniper's location.

are particularly good and ideal for the sniper. Even though this is the ideal option, a sniper care must be taken to avoid dependence on technology. He should also be aware that the laser beam emitted is visible – even the rapid-pulse type – to night optics under certain conditions and reveal your location to the enemy.

Many of the world's telescopic sights have range stadia as an integral part of the reticule, based upon the size of a man at various ranges. These are a quick and effective answer. Golfers use similar range finding gadgets which work from the size of the green flag at the hole. A golfer's range finder can be a cheap and effective aid for the sniper once he has worked out the comparison of the size of the flag to the size of a man.

JUDGING DISTANCE TRAINING

The basic starting point for distance training is to teach the sniper the importance of the skill and why reliance upon technology, whether it is available or not, is a bad thing. Then the sniper must be made aware of, and extensively practised in, the use of all of these methods of judging distance. With the reticule method, the sniper must be encouraged to create his own *aide-mémoir* of known heights for all battlefield scenarios. As well as measuring anything that may be found within the likely areas of operation, such as fence posts, three-bar gates and animal feed troughs in rural operations, or door frames, cars, phone boxes or windows in urban operations, a sniper must be encouraged to look up and note the relevant heights and widths of the vehicles and equipment of friend and foe. This must be done with an eye on the practical as the list of items to measure could be endless. Snipers should be advised that, prior to an operational deployment, it would be wise to study the area of potential deployment and the likely opposition, and create a relevant *aide-mémoir*. Even the depth of the average house brick can be of use; nothing should be disregarded. The

LEFT: The sniper will normally be issued some form of powerful spotting scope. But with larger magnification comes the problem of getting a stable image. The sniper therefore must be able to hold the optic as steady as possible in any position. By using the rifle and his body as a "platform" the sniper can effectively use his spotting scope whether standing, kneeling or sitting, ensuring stability whatever the terrain restrictions may be.

BELOW: Range estimation training must be practised over all types of terrain for the sniper to become effective. Here British snipers are being put through a range estimation training session in the bleak Falklands terrain where there are few objects to assist in the task in the way of size comparisons.

author has heard many keen but inexperienced sniper instructors rubbish the need for a sniper to be able to judge distance to a "gap in a hedgerow" or to a gatepost. But such estimates are vital to a sniper. The reason for this is that, in his appraisal of enemy's likely approach route, the sniper may deduce that the enemy will pass through that gap in the hedgerow or passed that fence post. If the range to these likely engagement points are pre-recorded on his range card the sniper will have the range target when the enemy appears.

To say that a sniper should only be trained to estimate range on to man-sized targets, because that's what he is going to shoot at, is completely wrong. The argument these people put forward is that the sniper will always have a map and can therefore measure the distance to any real estate feature with a protractor. While it is true that in certain armies the issue of accurate maps is much wider than, say, in World War II, it may not always be the case and the sniper must always train to the worst case scenario. Add to this that conflicts now take place in the urban settings and the availability of detailed maps of the inner city areas in the military is rare to say the least. Here the sniper will find himself estimating ranges using the known-height equation, so the need to know the height or width of everyday items will be of extreme importance.

To train snipers in this skill, the instructor will need to locate a piece of real estate with a good field of view and at least 1,100 yards (1,000m) in depth. Within this area there needs to be several natural and man-made features that can be readily indicated to the sniper at varying ranges from a specific observation point. The features can be at any angle to the observer and indeed the stand should, wherever possible, be a 6400 mil arc. The arc should allow for at least ten features for the sniper to estimate the range to, and some of these targets should be man-sized representations to practise range estimation for human targets.

The features should be indicated one at a time and the snipers allowed a reasonable amount of time to write down his estimate. If the sniper changes his mind, he can only change the answer if the instructor is present and initials it. The sniper is then shown the next feature and repeats the process. The features should be indicated in random order and not nearest to furthest or vice versa, as this would aid the sniper. The sniper can only change the answer of one question back from the question he is working on, to reduce the advantage later estimates may give him. The sniper must estimate the range to within plus or minus 15 per cent of the actual range in order for it to be marked correct, and he must achieve an overall grade of 70 per cent to pass the stand.

As the training and sniper's level of skill improves, the time allowed can be reduced and the start pass grade of 70 per cent can be raised by 5 per cent to maintain the level of concentration and avoid lethargy.

Judging distance is a vital skill to the sniper and every available opportunity to practise it should be used, whether it is in between shooting-range practices or at the airport awaiting deployment. It is one of the most perishable sniper skills and the author has met few snipers who can look at an object or person and accurately estimate the range to it.

SNIPER KNOWLEDGE

This rather broad heading covers all the areas of military training that are not vital to passing a basic sniper course, but are vital if the sniper is to be deployed and effective. The areas of military training that fall into this category are

BELOW: The author briefing Ghurkha snipers prior to the start of sniper training in the Falklands. The generally harsh weather conditions and barren terrain there make for a tough environment for the snipers, but they must be able to work in all weathers and any terrain throughout the world.

ABOVE: A Saab laser firing attachment attached to a British Army sniper rifle. This allows the sniper to engage targets across the battlefield during realistic training with "laser" bullets and prove his worth to exacting commanders.

many and varied and can change from deployment to deployment, but in general cover the following areas:

• Communication equipment and procedures.
• Equipment, uniform and tactics recognition.
• NBC (nuclear/biological/chemical) procedures and drills.
• Indirect fire control procedure.
• Forward air control procedure.
• Foreign weapon training.
• Combat pistol training.
• Close target reconnaissance procedure.
• Photography skills to include IR (infrared) photography.

Qualified snipers should have a competent working knowledge of these main topics, and this shows the very real necessity of programmed continuation training for all snipers. Often snipers are refused adequate time to train after they have passed a basic course, but the tests that a sniper must pass on a basic course are only the bare minimum. They mean that the soldier has reached a level where he is now suitable to be trained as an effective tool of war. Until he has been through continuation training, he is not the finished article.

COMMUNICATIONS

The sniper is only effective if he is in communication with his commander. Situations change quickly and the sniper

BELOW: The author briefs British and other NATO snipers on the day's training during the British Army "sniper concentration", an annual training event where all available snipers gather to train collectively and share tips and experiences.

needs to know if his tactical plan has been altered or if his rules of engagement have changed. This is never more important than in urban or internal security roles, where a change in the rules of engagement can mean the difference between a successful operation and a term in prison.

The sniper must be proficient with all communication equipment that he is likely to encounter and have a working knowledge of operating ranges, battery life and frequency variations. He must also be expert in radio procedures and the use of codes or encryption devices. Again all the training must be progressive in nature. Once the basics have been mastered the sniper must train with radio equipment as often as possible. Such things as carriage and stowage of spare batteries can only be handled through experience, trial and error, and may even lead to a change in the sniper's ghillie suit to accommodate the radio.

Radio procedure on such operations as a sniper ambush or a co-ordinated shoot are vital, and must be constantly practised if the skill is to be maintained. The difference between multi-rifle synchronised shooting and sporadic fire can be the difference between life and death.

RECOGNITION TRAINING

It stands to reason that if the sniper's main role is to kill the enemy, it is a major advantage if he can recognise them. To this end the sniper will undergo quite considerable recognition training on tactics, vehicles, weaponry, aircraft and uniforms of all the perceived enemies of his nation

Most armies produce very informative documents and manuals on foreign equipment and militaries. The sniper must be taught the most easily recognisable features of this equipment, from all angles, and be able to identify them.

BELOW: With snipers frequently working behind the enemy's lines they must be fully able to survive and escape back to their own lines. Here British snipers are taught the finer points of escape and evasion by a member of the British special forces.

This training takes the form of indoor lectures and written tests using video or slide footage, along with simulated longer-range training using Miltra models and issued optics. The range of vehicles and equipment in various scales that the Miltra company produce is excellent, and when viewed through optics at the proper distance can look very realistic. As with all training this needs to be regulated and progressive and can be made harder, by concealing more of the model, as the level of competency increases.

The reason an enemies tactics, SOPs (standard operating procedures) and vehicle formations are important is that, if he can identify a formation or a specific vehicle type, a sniper can draw further conclusions about the enemy's strengths and intentions. As this information is passed up the intelligence chain, a much larger picture may form, indicating an enemy's battle plan and its weaknesses.

In many armies, officers and specialists wear distinctive uniforms that can be used for identification by the sniper. Weaponry can also be used to identify individuals. For example, special forces often have weapons that regular soldiers don't have. This allows the sniper to identify special forces, and he can alert his commander via radio of the presence of these units. These recognition skills are essential if the sniper is to be effective and they must be taught to a very high level. Training by anti-tank and reconnaissance soldiers, who are expert in this area, can help.

When observing a group of soldiers, all outwardly dressed the same, trying to decide who to engage first in order to inflict the maximum damage is the sniper's first task. Subtle differences in clothing or weaponry will help the sniper pick out his target. But he has to know what he is looking for in the first place.

NBC PROCEDURES

The sniper is normally away from the main force, so he is out of reach of the collective alarms and the support of the unit's NBC capabilities. For this reason the sniper must be

highly skilled in all procedures and equipment relating to this demanding area of warfare. It is often said that the sniper is the ideal NBC sentry. With his forward position, he is ideally located to give an early warning of any attack. This is not true. The sniper has enough to contend with and cannot do his job effectively if hampered with other tasks.

INDIRECT FIRE CONTROL

With the sniper being both forward of the main force and concealed from the enemy's gaze, it is highly likely that he will see enemy movements and possibly large enemy formations. In this scenario the sniper can engage selected targets and inflict damage to the enemy's morale and command structure. But he can do only limited overall damage before the enemy conceals himself or the sniper is forced to withdraw to avoid enemy action. In these situations an accurate artillery or mortar barrage could cause untold damage to the enemy and it makes tactical sense to train snipers to call for and direct this type of fire. Indeed most armies train their snipers to carry out this task.

Although it is a fairly basic task, the drill needs to be practised if fire is to be delivered quickly and efficiently on

ABOVE: The author and fellow sniper during training in the Arizona desert. Both have the Accuracy International AW sniper rifle with extended light shields on the telescopic sights to reduce the sunlight reflection in the bright conditions of the area.

an unsuspecting enemy. As with many radio procedures in the military, the system for calling in supporting fire is a very simple one. This is to ensure that any soldier is capable of doing it even when under the stress of battle. Once communication with the support weapon commander has been established, the sniper provides the following information:

- The location of the target to be engaged. This will be either the target identification number, if it has been pre-recorded, or a grid reference, along with the sniper's own grid reference.
- The direction of the target, in mils, from your location.
- A description of the target. For example, "massed enemy personnel in the open".
- The type of fire required – neutralise, smoke or destroy.

Once the requested fire has arrived on target, changes may be needed to maximise the damage to the enemy. The sniper must be ready to rely any changes by radio. The fire is usually adjusted first for line – that is, moved to the left or right – then for range. To make matters easier, fire is usually adjusted by increments of 55 yards (50m).

Snipers can also use the firepower of modern main battle tanks to assist in the destruction of the enemy. There are three main ways to indicate a target to a tank crew:

- In person by speaking directly to one of the crew, but this requires you to move, exposed, to the tank.
- By using the tank telephone, but suffers from the same drawback as the previous method.
- By radio.

The sniper cannot use either of the first two methods since this would require him to expose his position to the enemy. So he must use the third option. The restriction of this method is that the sniper must convey to the tank crew exactly what it is that he wishes to be engaged. To do this he can use one or a combination of the following methods:

- Supply pre-recorded reference points.
- Use a shot from the tank in roughly the right direction as a reference.
- Use the direction of the tank barrel as a reference. For example: "Ref barrel, go half right, 440 yards [400m], farm building, base left side enemy machine gun."

Whichever method the sniper uses and whichever support weapon system is employed, the sniper must be proficient in both calling for and adjusting indirect fire. Although he can

ABOVE: A British Army sniper section wearing laser training sensors and firing units, deployed to play "enemy" snipers on a training exercise in Canada. Behind them is a Scimitar recce vehicle suitably modified to represent an aggressor tank.

cause immense damage to an enemy's morale and command structure on his own, a sniper's fire cannot compare with the damage done by a battery of twelve 155mm howitzers.

FORWARD AIR CONTROL
A sniper should have also the ability and the communications to call for and direct ground-attack aircraft. In reality however this rarely happens. The staggering cost of today's fighter aircraft means that they are too expensive to risk on assignments called in by lowly snipers. Most nations suffer an overall shortage of aircraft so you can understand why these assets are usually assigned to special forces or high command requests. Nevertheless it has to be said that the sniper is usually well placed to locate and identify valuable enemy targets and should be trained to call for air assets, even if he will rarely get them. The snipers of the US Marine Corps are trained in this fairly basic skill and are trusted to call for "fast air" if they have a suitable target – but then they have the planes to play with.

FOREIGN WEAPON TRAINING
The sniper will have already been trained to identify enemy units and personnel by the weapons they have and will from time to time find himself behind enemy lines. In these situations the sniper stands a better chance of survival if he has the ability to pick up and use effectively any enemy weapon he may come across. It will also help in his selection of priority targets if the sniper has a prior knowledge of an

enemy's weapons' capabilities because he has fired them. A lot of weapon manufacturers claim their systems are effective up to a given range. In reality, this is simply a sales ploy. Armed with the real capabilities of a weapon as a result of previous training with it, the sniper is at an advantage when assessing the risks posed by the weapons employed against him by his adversary. Any foreign weapon training should cover the basics of assembly, operation, sighting system, capabilities, magazine capacity and safe handling. Any sniper instructor should seize all opportunities to train his men on any weapon systems he can gain access to and, wherever possible, arrange frequent live-firing sessions to maintain his men's operational knowledge of those systems. The instructor should endeavour to acquire the enemy's sniper weapons and make his snipers carry out their qualification shoot using these weapons instead of their own. Whether the enemy's weapon is better or worse than his own, the snipers will have a clear understanding of the enemy sniper's capabilities. He will know at what ranges the enemy sniper is most likely to work, as the enemy will be restricted by the capabilities of the rifle he has been issued.

COMBAT PISTOL TRAINING

The majority of the world's sniper rifles are bolt action, and while it is possible to employ the technique of rapid bolt manipulation against multiple targets, the sniper is not going to get himself into a shooting match with the enemy at close range if he can help it. The sniper pair is in no way armed for a fight. Their biggest weapon is their ability to remain unseen, with one bolt-action rifle and one assault weapon between them. For the observer, the assault rifle will provide

ABOVE: A British Army sniper demonstrates setting up the Accuracy International AW rifle to his French counterpart during a British-run sniper training course held in France. Sharing knowledge with allies is useful.

BELOW: Using wooden props, A British Royal Marine sniper instructor oversees combat pistol training, essential for self-protection, during one of the "sniper concentration" events held annually in the UK.

him with an effective close-range weapon to defend himself, but for the sniper the long barrelled sniping rifle is less than ideal in these situations. For this reason the sniper is issued with a sidearm – be it an HK USP or a Browning HP, or indeed whichever weapon the sniper's army uses – for his own close protection.

This is another area of a sniper's training that is often overlooked. To suggest that snipers get combat pistol training usually draws the jibe: "Who do you think you are, the bloody SAS?" However, the sniper must be practised and proficient in the use of his sidearm. This training must start at the basic drill and shooting level and steadily progress up to combat shooting, utilising realistic scenarios and range periods. The situations in which the sniper is going to use his pistol are going to be of the close range type and could occur in any type of operation and terrain. To that end the sniper must be practised in all likely scenarios and the instructor must give the planning a great deal of thought to fully prepare the snipers for operational deployment.

The start point for training this weapon is the same as for any other – safe handling. Once mastered, the training should progress onto basic marksmanship training and range work. Only when the sniper can consistently hit targets using standard pistol techniques should the instructor move him on to more realistic training, with the sniper being taught how to draw the pistol from the holster quickly and efficiently, and bring the weapon to bear in the shortest time, adopt and fire from alternative positions, fire round and through different types of cover, fire on the move, shoot over longer ranges and to use such shooting methods as the "double tap". To neglect or to take short cuts in this area of a sniper's training is to risk losing him on operations. The sniper will always be at risk of a chance encounter or infiltration past an enemy position, so the likelihood of coming into close combat is very real. To dismiss the need for sniper's sidearm training could easily lead to the sniper's death.

CLOSE TARGET RECONNAISSANCE

Close target reconnaissance is usually carried out by the dedicated recce troops of a unit and wherever possible, it should be left to them. But the sniper should still be able to carry out this task both to assist where needed, and to recce likely sniper and hide locations as a part of his own operational deployment. The similarities between the sniper's role and that of the reconnaissance soldier are often confused. The sniper does not necessarily make a good recce soldier. Likewise the reconnaissance soldier does not necessarily make a good sniper. However, they complement each other when deployed correctly.

The sniper is trained to a much higher standard in concealment and observation than the recce soldier and his ability to move very close to an enemy and remain unseen is also better. The reason for this is that he has a different role from the recce soldier. The reconnaissance soldier works in a team of four. Although he will endeavour to remain undetected at all times, his principal role is to observe and support. Snipers, on the other hand, work in pairs and, although they will be looking for a position from which to observe and report, their ultimate aim is to engage the enemy.

Over the course of his career, the author has been both sniper and reconnaissance soldier. Without a doubt, the

BELOW: A British Army Gurkha sniper pair advances cautiously along a riverbed while stalking during training in the Falklands. The snipers are taught to maximise the use of available dead ground when moving, a skill that is vital, particularly in the bare terrain of the Falklands.

ABOVE: A Slovenian sniper instructor explains some specific points while training one of his students. The instructor himself was trained in the United Kingdom, and the combination of East and West is evident in the ghillie suit and camouflaged Russian-made Dragunov sniper rifle.

sniper's training is much harder. But it is recommended that snipers and their instructors attend a reconnaissance course or cross train with reconnaissance soldiers so that they can fully understand each other's jobs and appreciate how best to support each other on operations. However, the techniques of close target reconnaissance are many and varied, and too detailed to be included in this chapter. It is also a secondary role for the sniper and does not warrant expanding here. But it is essential for the sniper both to understand the role and know how best to work along side his reconnaissance counterpart.

PHOTOGRAPHY

A high quality photograph is much better than a hand-drawn sketch from a sniper, especially as the photographic images can now be transmitted electronically back from the battlefield almost instantaneously. So it makes tactical sense to train the sniper in the finer arts of photography. However, as intelligence gathering is a secondary task of the sniper, there is a very real risk of overloading him with high tech kit that he will probably not use. On the other hand, it pays to make the most of his superior concealment skills in all phases and types of warfare. In the internal security role when one is dealing with a hostile public, it can be useful to infiltrate snipers into the area to carry out a photo reconnaissance of a target. After dark they can be moved forward to photo-

graph at close range, or even the inside, an area for future operations, using infrared photography. They already have the training perform this infiltration without alerting the locals, before withdrawing to a pre-arranged pick-up point. When it comes to photography, snipers do not have to be trained to professional paparazzi levels, merely to be able to take clear readable photographs whenever the need arises.

NAVIGATION

The sniper must be able to move across any piece of real estate and use that ground to its maximum advantage. He must be a very competent navigator. The student selected to attend a basic sniper course should already be adept with a map and compass, be able to interpret information from a map and move himself from one place to another. The sniper course then builds on this and adds the skills of map ground studies and map route selection. The sniper is expected to navigate over any terrain with precision and use the lay of the ground to his advantage day or night – bearing in mind that the world is a very different place when you are crawling.

The sniper is also taught a very old, yet mostly forgotten, skill of air photography interpretation. The use of air photographs for planning and navigation is usually restricted to the likes of special forces or dedicated intelligence units. At the level of the foot soldier, it has been all but lost. The tools of the trade and skills involved have not changed at combat troop level since World War II. Indeed the standard-issue stereoscope used by the British Army to transform a photo into a three dimensional image is the same type used to plan the Normandy landings and Operation Market Garden at Arnhem.

ABOVE: Snipers must be expert navigators and spend many hours learning to read both maps and aerial photographs. Here, British snipers conduct ground-to-map studies from a suitable piece of high ground in Northern Ireland.

BELOW: A British sniper pauses to check his map during a stalk against an "enemy" OP. His partner is covering him from further back in the woodline while he is vulnerable to surprise by the enemy.

The advantage of having an up-to-date image of the ground to be covered at the planning stage is one that cannot be overstated, as a photo will provide information that a map simply cannot. The photo will show local foliage, human activity in the area, obstacles, possible routes and many other snippets of information not found on any map. With a sequential set of air photos and a stereoscope, the sniper has the advantage of not only seeing the ground from a bird's eye view, but also the actual lay of the land with dead ground, gradients and intervisibility. These things are all visible with the air photo transformed in to a three-dimensional image. The seasonal changes in nature, with drastic changes in density and colour of foliage, are vitally important to the sniper who relies on nature to conceal him from the enemy. The availability of both black-and-white and colour air photos at the planning stage of a sniper's mission will enable him to plan his route in detail and make any colour changes to his ghillie suit that may be required.

The sniper will be taught to grid and scale an air photo to enable it to be used for accurate navigation and to allow for the accurate recording of information such as distances from object to object and details of enemy defences as part of intelligence gathering. The advantages of a combination of map and air photograph are obvious and the sniper is taught to use them with maximum efficiency in battle.

CAMOUFLAGE AND CONCEALMENT TRAINING

The sniper's main weapon in any phase of war is his ability to remain undetected, so the levels of training in camouflage and concealment must be of the highest standard. No lowering of these standards can be allowed or tolerated. The standards were set by men who spent time under all-out war conditions. They set them because they worked, so to lower them because of high failure rate or because the soldier of today cannot cope with such demanding conditions is ludicrous. If one man can pass, the standards cannot be too high for today's soldier. A high failure rate simply means a failure in the selection process, so the problem lies with the command structure and not the would-be sniper.

This area of sniper training is another where inexperienced but keen individuals often fail to fully appreciate the reasoning behind some of the training standards and feel that they need modifying. They do not. The ability to disappear into any type of foliage at a moment's notice is key to a sniper's survival, as the sniper is not always going to have time to select and prepare his position. When stalking, the sniper will have already selected a probable firing position from his map and air photo study. Assuming that he arrives at this point undetected, he will spend time and effort preparing both the position and himself to ensure that his camouflage is of the highest standards. This will aid his continued concealment from the enemy when he announces his presence with a shot. However, the same time and effort will not be available if the sniper has a chance encounter with an enemy patrol on route to his firing position and to survive he will have to conceal himself in a very short space of time. This possibility is reproduced in the sniper's training with the concealment stand, where the sniper will be given a clearly defined area in which he must conceal himself while maintaining a shooting position on a designated target. He will then be given only a matter of a few minutes to hide within that arc before the "enemy" starts to look for him using binoculars.

Critics of this method point out that it is unrealistic to expect the sniper to conceal himself in three to seven min-

ABOVE: British snipers train for multiple engagements or the sniper ambush, where several snipers combine to devastate an enemy with multiple precision casualties. Here range restrictions keep them a lot closer than they would be in reality.

BELOW: A sniper instructor averts his eyes as students race to conceal themselves in a given arc. With just three minutes to hide, they simulate the possibility of "enemy pre-seen" and rapidly conceal themselves before they are spotted.

ABOVE: French instructors observe for snipers concealed in a given area of real estate, with a British sniper instructor overseeing the lesson. To the rear of the Brit are snipers who have already been seen and have failed the test.

BELOW: The lonely life of the sniper instructor! An instructor moves away from the OP to act as the OP's "walker" while observing for snipers during training. The snow will make it harder for the snipers but weather never stops training.

utes, as they feel that this does not reflect operational eventualities. However, these same instructors teach SOPs and "Actions On" to all soldiers and JNCOs (Junior NCOs) from military doctrine that covers orders for all combat situations. Within every set of these orders there is a section headed "Actions on enemy pre-seen", or what to do if you come across the enemy unexpectedly and he is going to see you very soon if you do nothing. This is exactly the same scenario that the sniper is training for when involved in a concealment stand, so it is very realistic to expect a soldier, who is dependent upon his ability to remain unseen, to conceal himself in any terrain and in a very short space of time.

The concealment stand will cover a piece of training ground that offers a variety of foliage and gradients that will be broken down into three distinct arcs. Each arc should offer the sniper several choices of cover in which to conceal himself up to 330 yards (300m) from the OP (observation position) and between 500 and 3200 mils in width. In the OP will be a sniper instructor who, at the end of the allotted time, will look for the snipers with a standard-issue pair of x7 magnification binoculars. Any sniper that is located is identified by the observer directing a "walker" by radio onto that sniper's location. The walker is not on the observer's side or the sniper's. He is there to act as a judge between the two. If the observer cannot place get the walker to place his hand on the sniper, the sniper carries on with the test as the observer obviously cannot see the sniper well enough to fail him. If, however, the observer can direct the walker's hand onto the sniper, the sniper fails and is removed from the arc.

If after a nominated length of time the observer cannot locate the sniper, the sniper will move on to the next phase of the stand. At this stage the observer will instruct the walker to move to within 11 yards (10m) of the sniper's position. The observer will study this area for a set amount of time. If the sniper is then located, the same procedure will

ABOVE: The "walker's" hand is being guided by the observer in the OP on to what he believes is the sniper. The OP was spot on and the sniper failed the test.

RIGHT: An instructor radios a sniper as to why the OP has located him. In this case the sniper had failed to apply natural foliage to his ghillie suit.

be used with the walker being directed by radio onto the sniper's position and the sniper fails. If the sniper is still undetected the walker will point directly at the sniper while the observer watches. Again if seen he fails, if not he moves on with the test.

Next the sniper is instructed to fire a blank shot at the observer while the observer looks directly at his position. If seen as a result of his shot, such as foliage moving with the weapon blast and indicating his position, then the sniper fails. If he is still unseen he will be asked to identify a letter or number board held up across the body by the observer to prove that he does actually have line of sight onto the target and that he is not just lying below the level of the observer's vision. The reason for this, and why the sniper is just not allowed to simply slip into dead ground, is because in combat once you have made contact with the enemy, whether he

ABOVE: To prove that the sniper is actually aiming at the OP and not simply lying in dead ground, the sniper must correctly identify a letter or number board held up briefly by the instructor in the OP. His instructors are extremely demanding; failure in "real life" could be fatal for the sniper and his partner, and other friendly forces.

BELOW: Apparently well concealed, this trainee sniper has failed to conceal the outline of his telescopic sight. It forms a tunnel effect that draws the attention of an expert observer, who then can locate the circular end to his barrel. On a real battlefield, that's all an enemy sniper would need to shoot his counterpart or draw down supporting fire on him.

is active or passive, you must remain in contact with him. That way, you can see what he is doing, you know where he is and what he might do next. If you do not, the enemy can easily surprise you should he reappear from an unexpected direction. The test is designed to reflect this.

If the sniper cannot identify the board, he fails. If he can, the final part of the test is the checking, by the walker, of the range estimation and wind strength estimation on the sniper's sight drums. If correct, he passes the arc; if wrong, he fails. During the stand the sniper will complete three arcs and, to pass the stand, he must pass two out of the three arcs.

This test has recently been changed by the Royal Marines and now only has one arc with a straight pass or fail. An argument against this change would be that you can be lucky with one arc, but to pass two out of three requires skill – and that, after all, is what we are looking for. The old system worked fine. Why change it?

STALKING

Movement catches the eye. Indeed movement defies the principles of concealment, so for the sniper to be effective he must do the impossible. He must be able to cross any piece of real estate, in full view of the enemy, and remain unseen, be that enemy 880 yards (800m) away or 220 yards (200m) away. It is for this reason that the sniper must be able to master all seven of the sniper skills, as they all go together to enable the sniper to carry out a successful stalk.

The sniper will spend a good deal of time planning his stalk and using the ground to his advantage. This tends to involve a lot of crawling which, in turn, will increase the chances of the enemy stumbling upon the sniper with little warning. So the sniper will look to use any advantage he find. The sniper will break down his route into sections and will move from cover to cover along that route, constantly stopping to listen and look for the enemy, and to adjust his camouflage to suit the cover available in the next section or bound. On each bound he will assume that the area is under enemy observation and move with extreme caution, utilising any natural features that will conceal him, or any distractions that may divert the enemy attention away from him. But his movement and route will always be influenced by time needed to complete his task and he must allow for this at the planning stage.

Before deploying on any stalk, the sniper will carry out an appreciation of the task, and he will make a detailed map and air photo study of the area as the likelihood of observing the actual ground to be covered is slight. The sniper will

ABOVE: A Gurkha sniper moves carefully and slowly along some shallow dead ground in his approach to his Final Fire Position (FFP). He keeps the optic lens of his sight covered to avoid accidental light reflection.

BELOW: A British sniper instructor indicates the area of the "enemy" OP to snipers prior to deploying on a training stalk. The snipers will then plan and execute their route to a fire position from which to engage the enemy.

seek out the following information to assist in his overall concept of operations:

- The enemy location to be engaged.
- Enemy strengths and dispositions within his area of operation.
- Probable final fire positions, obtained from an assessment of the enemy and the ground to be covered.
- Routes in and out of the area.
- Support available while on task.

The route in and out are of vital importance to the sniper's safe return and will be carefully planned from all available information. Once committed to a route, it may be impossible to change it. The route will be broken down into bounds and each bound will be carefully studied on the ground before the sniper enters it and modification will be made within operational restrictions if needs be. The sniper will be looking for the following information when planning:

- Likely fire positions.
- Possible vantage points along his route from which to observe the next bound.
- Obstacles either man-made or natural.
- Available cover, and hence the type of movement possible for that bound, and estimated time needed to cross it.
- Dead ground.
- Any obvious landmarks that will aid navigation while crawling.
- Civilian dispositions within the area.
- Animal dispositions within the area.
- Possible withdrawal routes.

ABOVE: A sniper uses a tree to conceal him from the "enemy" and raise his position to facilitate a better view over his next bound on the stalk. Again, the evident snow and cold do not restrict training. "If it ain't raining, it ain't training!"

Once the sniper has completed his plan he will deploy. It is essential that all friendly troops are aware of the sniper's departure, release point and the estimated time and area of his return to avoid any friendly fire. The most vulnerable time for the sniper is when departing his own lines. He has no way of knowing if the enemy has that area under observation and may be moving straight into an ambush. From that moment on, he and his partner are on their own.

During the stalk the sniper must maintain a sense of direction. This is achieved with the compass and by using visible reference points along the way. The pair must remain alert at all times. To relax is to invite death and the mental strain of this type of deployment is very high. The snipers must stop and observe the area constantly during the stalk and, if in doubt, wait until they can be sure of the next bound. A dead sniper is of no use to his commander. If any risks are to be taken during the stalk, it is advisable to take them early on when the snipers are furthest from the enemy. The closer the snipers get, the slower they move. If the snipers suspect they could have been seen, they must instinctively chose between freezing where they are, and hope that the lack of movement will put the enemy off their position, or moving quickly to the nearest hard cover and extracting. A sniper's personnel camouflage will need to be changed or adjusted several times during a stalk to suit the type of foliage he is moving through, and the pair will work together to ensure that nothing is overlooked or mistakes made that will betray them to an observing enemy.

ABOVE: Resembling "abominable snowmen", a sniper pair moves into a woodline to maximise the effect of their ghillie suits under the snowy conditions. The specially constructed suits, while almost comical looking to the camera, will offer very effective concealment in the correct environment.

The pair will generally use the same lines of advance and will operate a maximum of around 28 yards (25m) apart, with one man moving while the other covers him. They co-ordinate their movement with hand signals to keep noise levels to a minimum. During the stalk, the pair may use a variety of movement techniques depending upon the time and cover available.

THE WALK

A walk is to patrol upright with the weapon in the shoulder at the ready position. This reduces the time it takes to bring the weapon into action if the enemy is encountered. The movement is slow and the feet are placed down with the outside of the foot touching ground first, then slowly rolling the rest of the foot down to avoid the noise of breaking twigs or rustling leaves. This method provides quicker movement over ground and is less tiring than others, but the sniper must display caution and avoid moving too fast.

THE MONKEY RUN

This involves the sniper moving while on his hands and knees with the weapon supported in one hand; the other is used in conjunction with the knees to move forward. This is used when the cover is thick but low. It is tiring and potentially noisy.

THE LEOPARD CRAWL

This is the flat crawl that every child can do and everyone has seen demonstrated in war movies. It is used to cross low cover or in limited dead ground with the weapon either carried in both hands or supported over one arm while crawling.

THE STOMACH CRAWL

This is a modification of the leopard crawl, the primary difference being that the stomach stays on the ground with the body propelled using the hands and feet only to push the sniper along. It is very time consuming and tiring, and is used when close to the enemy or at high-risk areas.

ABOVE: The basic, tiring and time-consuming "leopard crawl", the main method of movement in very low vegetation or when close to the enemy.

BELOW: The "stomach crawl", a modified "leopard crawl" but slower and lower to the ground. The body is propelled using the hands and feet only.

ABOVE: A sniper illustrating "the walk". The rifle (shown uncamouflaged for clarity) is in the alert position to allow a rapid discharge of shot.

BELOW: The "monkey run" method of moving, supporting the rifle in one hand and moving the body with the other. It would be used in low vegetation.

ABOVE: Here the sniper illustrates a different method of weapon carriage while using the "stomach crawl. Instead of the weapon being under the body, it is carried out in front across both hands. (Again, for clarity here, it is not camouflaged.)

Throughout the stalk the sniper pair must be aware of their surroundings at all times and maintain a 6,400mil threat arc, as you cannot assume that the enemy will only appear from the one direction. During the stalk, the pair must also monitor their surroundings for any signs of the enemy, while applying a series of movement principles. These principles can be remembered by using the pneumonic **PW-CAMDRASS.**

P. Ploughed fields should be avoided and if they have to be crossed then move along a furrow to avoid leaving signs on the ground.

W. Wildlife must be it avoided or used as an aid to enemy detection.

C. Camouflage must be monitored and changed accordingly with each bound.

A. Action, or sequence of actions for each bound: observe, listen, move, halt, observe.

M. Movement must suit the type of foliage you are moving in with both speed and type of movement considered.

D. Directional changes should be included in your bound at irregular intervals to avoid leaving a clear path to follow, and when moving through long grass to avoid any unnatural movement of the grass. The best time to move through long grass is in strong wind, as the grass will be moving irregular patterns.

R. Roads should only be crossed if unavoidable and they should be crossed at low points or dips in the road, or at curves or bends where visibility is limited, or ideally through drains or culverts.

A. Advantage of noise or distractions, such as weather, artillery fire, heavy traffic, low flying aircraft or anything that will cover the noise of your movement.

S. Steep slopes, areas of loose soil or cleared areas should be avoided if possible as movement within these areas will quickly draw attention.

S. Silhouetting should be guarded against at all times; this includes both avoiding ridges where you can be sky-lined, and avoiding being silhouetted against your backdrop because your camouflage is wrong.

If the sniper applies these principles whenever he is moving, he should never get caught out or find himself in a fire fight with superior enemy forces. The stalking of an enemy is not only very dangerous but also very demanding in both physical and mental terms. The stalk demands constant alertness and for the sniper to mentally update his position

BELOW: A French officer during sniper training peers cautiously along his next bound before committing to movement. He is carrying the French FRF2 rifle and is wearing a ghillie suit, the latter showing a British influence.

STALK TASK APPRECIATION

Considerations	Left	Centre	Right	Remarks + Discuss
Fire Positions				
View of Trg Area				
Natural Bounds				
Good Cover				
Dead Ground				
Landmarks				
Obstacles				
Area to Observe				
Withdrawal Routes				
TOTALS				

Conclusions:

_____

_____

_____

_____

_____

LEFT: A German sniper adopts the standing position to use the weapon optic to observe the ground to his front. He is taking part in a British sniper instructor course prior to moving to the newly formed German Army sniper school.

ABOVE: An issued stalk options form used by the sniper to deliberate on all of his options. Such a document will help him avoid the tendency to opt for perhaps the first and most obvious choice, which is not always the best!

in relation to what the enemy can and cannot see, to out-manoeuvre and out-think his prey. The skills of observation, navigation, concealment, camouflage, judging distance and shooting all mould together to make the successful stalk. To fail in one area is to fail the mission. It is for this reason that the basic sniper course lays down the ruling that to fail one subject is to fail the course. This rule is designed to avoid sending unsuitable men to their deaths.

The selection and training of snipers is a very demanding one, and the correct resources and time must be allocated if the unit is to have professional men to deploy. To skip on any of these areas will lead to a unit having poorly trained men who will embarrass the unit on exercise, and be lost to enemy action on operations. The command structure of any unit that is established to deploy snipers would be well advised to plan and conduct a thorough selection and basic course, and to allow the unit sniper instructor to train to the correct levels by committing to the high standards required at the early stages. That way, in the long run, the unit commander will have a valuable asset to deploy.

CAMOUFLAGE AND CONCEALMENT

The sniper, more than any other soldier, realises the need to remain unseen, for to be discovered means almost certain death. Throughout history we can see the progressive strides man has made to hide himself from his prey, be it hunting animals in order to eat, or hunting each other in order to dominate. The Native Americans used buffalo skins draped over themselves to approach herds without alerting them to their presence, but it was a long time before man realised that he stood a better chance of surviving in combat if his opponent could not see him.

This realisation was directly linked to the advances in accuracy of the weapons that soldiers used against each other, since they found it was becoming too dangerous to advance on the enemy with drums beating and dressed in red! As the world's armies moved to more unobtrusive colours for their uniforms, the art of sniping was preparing to enter centre stage. The arrival of the sniper in World War I led to many advances in camouflage on the battlefield, ranging from snipers' suits to complete dummy trees, with both sides employing recognised artists to add to the overall quality.

The art of camouflage can be described as "making an object unobtrusive or unrecognisable by imitation or deception", and the best method to use is always that which nature has provided. The sniper very quickly learned that "nature has all the answers". Wherever possible, the best way for a sniper to remain unseen is to not draw attention to himself, and the best way to do that is to match his surroundings in both shape and colour. To achieve this he must apply the following when planning his camouflage:

- Minute attention to detail.
- Forethought and imagination.
- Study of any air photographs, maps or other photos of the area of operation.

For the sniper this attention to detail starts with his own clothing and equipment, and this usually means his ghillie suit. The ghillie suit is a form of clothing adopted by the British and subsequently used by most of the world's snipers. Its origins can be traced back to the estate wardens or gamekeepers of the old Scottish estates who used this form of camouflage to both keep a close eye on the deer and also to help them in the fight against the poachers that plagued the estates. The combined skills of long range observation and camouflage that the ghillies (as the keepers were called) possessed were put to good use by Lord Lovat when he formed them into the British Army unit known as the Lovat Scouts. These men were drafted into the newly forming sniper schools to act as field craft instructors, and with them they brought the ghillie suit, and the archetypal image of a sniper was born.

The fact that sniping is a very individual skill, in that what works for one sniper may not suit another, means that

BELOW: A British Army sniper pair engages a target. Note the close proximity of the observer to allow for adjustments if needed and the netting shroud used to conceal the optic lens of the scope. The limited camouflage applied to the rifle in no way affects the weapon's accuracy.

each ghillie suit will vary to a greater or lesser degree from another. The differences can be something as small as an additional pocket up to the complete design and construction of the suit. Today there are many wide and varied options of man-made camouflage to choose from, but for a suit that will provide camouflage over a wide spectrum the first choice of most experienced snipers is one constructed using hessian (burlap). Hessian is the material used in the construction of army-issue sandbags and this is indeed where most snipers gather the material from.

Although the trade of a sniper is now well established, the equipment and materials the sniper uses are still a combination of the issued, the improvised and the stolen, partly due to the individualistic nature of the trade and more usually due to the lack of investment in the role by the world's armies. The reluctance to recognise the importance of snipers, even today, is all too common and this lack of belief in and understanding of the capabilities of well-trained snipers means that the full range and employment options of snipers are very rarely if ever realised.

The advantage of using hessian in the suit is mainly due to the fact that the material "weathers" so well after it has become wet and dirty. The sniper will either unpick the material to give its "shaggy" appearance, or will brush it with a mechanic's wire brush to achieve the same effect. The reason the suit works so well is that the eye operates in combination with the memory: when we scan an area we are

ABOVE: This French Special Forces soldier is wearing a ghillie suit he has made from a camouflaged parachute. While it makes a very light suit, the material does not weather in the way that Hessian does, and in the field the result proves to be more of a liability than a good idea!

BELOW LEFT AND RIGHT: A British sniper in a commercially made netting jacket that many snipers are now using. The jacket has green elastic already attached and the sniper merely adds the Hessian as he sees fit. Combined with trousers it provides a lightweight and easily packed ghillie suit.

ABOVE AND BELOW: A detailed examination of the sniper's net jacket reveals it to be waist length at the front but with a longer tail at the rear, a feature designed to assist in the sniper's overall concealment. The light coloured patches evident in the photo are the remains of dried glue which has been used to attach the hessian.

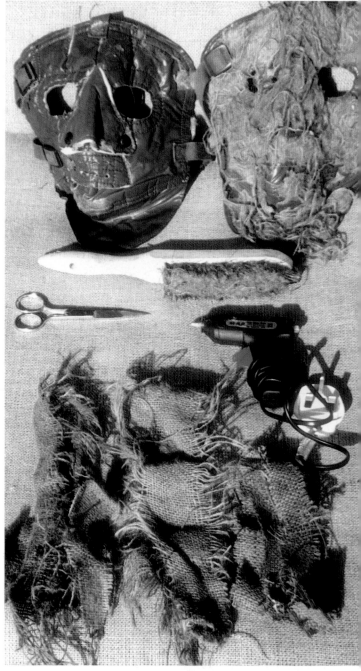

ABOVE: All you need to make a ghillie suit! The construction is easy but time consuming. At the top of the photo are two US tank drivers' cold weather masks often used by snipers to conceal the face, one before and one during the application of Hessian. Prime components are: Hessian, a glue gun and sticks, scissors and a wire brush to "weather" the hessian.

looking for things that the memory can recognise, so if the sniper adopts a natural or un-human-like appearance, then he goes unseen. The ghillie suit presents the eye with a lack of defined shapes with which to build an assessment on, and as a result usually goes unnoticed. This obvious advantage works only if the attention to detail, which is so important to a sniper, has been considered in the suit's construction.

The construction of the suit needs as much forethought and imagination as the planning of any future operation in which it will be worn. The fauna of the general area of operation and the primary colours to be found there must all be taken into consideration. If the hessian is not available in the required colour, then the sniper must consider dyeing it before applying it to his suit. An unnatural colour is as obvious to a trained observer as an unnatural shape, and while it is never going to be possible to adapt to every type of area of operation, it is essential to identify the main theatre of likely operations and its predominant colours, and apply them in the suit construction.

The suit is without doubt an excellent aid to concealment, but it is not the whole answer, and it certainly does not make a man invisible. The sniper must allow ample space to apply natural vegetation to correspond with that in the area in which he finds himself. This is achieved by attaching green elastic to the suit, or some other secure means of attaching fauna, since the only way to succeed is to emulate nature. This means using a combination of ghillie suit and vegetation.

Why green elastic? Well, the easiest elastic to purchase on the open market is black, but since there are very few if any naturally black areas of vegetation, to attach this to the suit is to court death. A trained observer or indeed another

ABOVE: A well-camouflaged sniper pauses during a stalk to observe and listen for sounds of the enemy. Note the way that his suit and the application of natural foliage help to him to blend well into his surroundings.

BELOW: A close up view of the sniper's headdress reveals the green elastic to facilitate the attaching of natural vegetation to aid concealment. This must be attached in different aspects to allow for a "natural" appearance from all angles.

well-trained sniper will spot black objects no matter how small or apparently insignificant. Most of the world's snipers are issued with at least a x10 magnification optical sight or pair of binoculars with which to search and scan, so what would appear to be of little importance could well be enough to get the target sniper killed.

This accentuates why the phrase "attention to detail" is so important in the field of sniping; for any sniper who believes that all this is too much effort or unnecessary, there is a sniper who does not, waiting to kill him in some future conflict. A good sniper believes there is always someone better than him; the trick is never to meet him, but if he does, why make it easy for him by not paying enough attention to preparation?

The choice of either an all-in-one type coverall (flight suit) or a two-piece jacket and trousers for the construction of the ghillie suit is one of personal preference, but there are certain considerations to take into account. First, the clothing must be hardy enough to withstand the rigours of prolonged crawling and contact with Mother Nature. A flimsy article will very quickly be destroyed, no matter how good the sniper may look in it. Most snipers will modify issued uniforms or suitable civilian options, as these tend to be hard-wearing.

The next step is to ensure that the suit allows the freedom of movement to carry out all the tasks associated with sniping, such as crawling, climbing and adopting the many and varied shooting positions without restriction in any way. Again, the idea is to be effective and not just to look good on the firing ranges. As a general rule, bigger is better.

Once the base clothing has been selected and tried out for freedom of movement, the sniper needs to consider the

ABOVE: Although this sniper has broken up his outline, he has failed to match the colours of his surroundings and hence is highly visible. Colour is vitally important for concealment.

RIGHT: A British ghillie suit showing the variously angled green elastic and the attachment of small pouches to allow the sniper to carry his most often used kit where he most needs it.

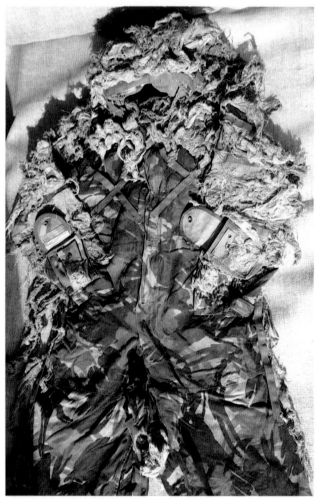

operational equipment that he will have to carry upon his person, and where he wishes to store it. This will almost certainly involve repositioning the pockets that are already on the clothing, since they are rarely in the right places for a sniper. The reason for this is that a sniper spends most of his time on his stomach, so any pockets on the front of his clothing will hinder his smooth movement across the ground or affect the stability and comfort of shooting positions. He also does not wish to make any large movements to reach kit in his pockets, since movement catches the eye, so the pockets need to be placed on the suit in such a way as to facilitate minimum movement. This tends to be on the forearms for equipment such as lightweight compass or secateurs, and on the side or back for larger items.

The sniper will try and modify the suit accordingly to ensure he deploys on operations with a working system, and further modifications will most definitely be required dependent upon task or terrain. The ghillie suit for all terrains does not exist, so the sniper will be required to have more than one, or at least one that has the scope for modification.

The addition of pockets or small pouches from other clothing is not uncommon, and this all leads to a very unorthodox appearance. But the sniper is an unorthodox sol-

ABOVE: A Gurkha sniper attaches natural vegetation to his ghillie suit prior to deployment. He may change it many times during a stalk as he moves through different areas.

RIGHT: A British sniper moves into a fire position, using the longer grass to his front as a screen from instructors in the OP at the base of the smaller tree top left of the picture.

dier and one who is not confined by the need to be smart on a parade square as well as effective in battle, all in the same uniform. The final set-up of pockets on the suit can only come about through trial and error, and advice from other snipers. But if the sniper gets it wrong or overlooks it, he will pay for it later, either having to spend many hours modifying his suit, or worst of all, losing his life.

Having reached the stage of selecting his preferred choice of clothing and moving the pockets accordingly, the sniper can now attach the elastic. This is usually done with a simple do-it-yourself glue gun, or alternatively the tried and tested method of sewing it on individually. Whichever method is used, the sniper must again picture how vegetation grows in comparison to the positions that he is likely to adopt, and then attach the elastic to the suit to allow him to emulate this in the way he applies fauna to his person. If all the surrounding vegetation is growing up towards the sun, and all that he attaches to himself is horizontal because of the way he has applied the elastic in his suit construction, he will very quickly be located and killed. So it is essential that he applies the elastic, or preferred attachment alternative, in several different planes or directions to facilitate the application of natural camouflage that will be effective whether he is moving upright or crawling.

With the pockets and elastic applied it is now time to attach the hessian to the suit. The main areas to apply hessian are the head, shoulders, back and arms, as these are the areas that are mainly going to be in view of an enemy. The front of the suit is mainly left clear with the exception of the front of the shoulders down to the level of the top of the ribs. This is to ensure that the hessian does not hook up on any vegetation while the sniper is crawling. While a sniper will spend most of his time in the prone or crawling position, for the remainder of the time he will operate on a route that will maximise his ability to use the natural cover available to conceal him while moving upright. Therefore the hessian attachment to the front of the suit should be such that it breaks up the outline of the head and shoulders only. To attach it any further down will almost certainly restrict movement, and if any piece of real estate has to be crossed close to an enemy, then the sniper is going to be crawling and the hessian and natural camouflage covering his back will do the job.

To apply the hessian, the material should be cut into 2-inch (50mm) wide strips of approximately 12 inches (300mm) in length and either sewn or stuck on using the DIY glue gun. The strips should be applied so that they overlap and cover the clothing, but care must be taken not to

ABOVE: A sniper pair use dead ground of tank ruts to conceal their movement across an open field. The use and identification of dead ground is a vital skill to the sniper.

BELOW: A sniper who has allowed himself to be silhouetted against his backdrop because he does not match the colour and would hence be seen. He should have crawled.

overdo the application. During the process the suit should be put on and checked in a mirror for gaps in coverage, or better still the advice of a more experienced sniper should be sought. The overall coverage is again a thing of personal preference, but in general one layer should be applied and then checked, adding or cutting off as appropriate.

The colour of the hessian applied is going to be dictated by the general terrain the sniper is likely to work in, but he should try always to apply lighter colours as opposed to darker. The reason for this is that a sniper is invariably wet, due to the nature of the job, and this means that his clothing will assume a slightly darker shade due to the water. If he has chosen darker colours in the first place his suit is now going to be even darker, and as a consequence he will present any observer with a very dark area of vegetation that will undoubtedly raise his suspicions. Applying light colours in the construction stage leaves the option of going darker by using natural foliage if required; the sniper can always go darker but not lighter, so it is sensible to err on the side of caution.

The choice of camouflage that can be bought already applied to military-type clothing is ever increasing, but for the professional sniper I would strongly suggest avoiding all the hype and glamour of the different commercial options and spend the time and effort in constructing his own ghillie suit in the tried and tested way. The reason for this is very simple: while many of the civilian hunter camouflage styles that are available are indeed very good at fooling animals, snipers are not chasing game – they are up against a *man*, possibly another sniper.

ABOVE: A sniper must use whichever camouflage he feels will best suit his area of operations and there are many to choose from. Each has advantages and disadvantages and the selection for his ghillie suit construction must be well thought out. Here we have, left to right: German Fleck tarn, Sierra Leone, early Austrian, British DPM, Russian and French.

LEFT: As with general areas of operations there are also several options on more specific areas, such as the desert environment. Here again we have a selection of different camouflage options that a sniper can consider. Left to right: French, German, British and second-generation American with the original "chocolate chip" pattern on the backing to the uniforms.

Many of the "real tree" type camouflage patterns are superb while the wearer is static inside a tree line, but a sniper is very rarely static. Indeed, sniper doctrine states that he should take no more than two shots from any one position before moving. It can be seen therefore that these types of camouflage would have limited use in the world of the military sniper. That is not to say that they should be instantly discounted, since a successful sniper is one that keeps an open mind and adopts his plan to suit the situation, and there may come a time when that option would be the only one that offered a chance of success.

There are also several advertised alternative ghillie suits using some of the new materials on the market, but these do present problems when considered for the military sniper. The main problem for all of these new materials is that they do not weather in the way that hessian does, and the construction of the suits is too cumbersome for operational use. There are various European military special forces who have been photographed in these types of suit, and the photos suggest that they employ them operationally. I have to draw the conclusion that within these units there is a lack of operational experience in the field of sniping, since all experienced snipers know that these proprietary suits and materials do not work when going up against anything other than low-level opposition. The end user of these suits is usually inexperienced or looking for an easy option to constructing a ghillie suit. Take my word for it: there isn't one.

While the civilian market is of limited use to the professional sniper at present, snipers should always keep a close eye on future developments. The practice of looking for anything that can be adapted or that would make the sniper's job easier from anywhere within the military or civilian market is one that any sniper should be encouraged to adopt. Many times a civilian item, not intended for military use, can be just the thing you are looking for, and the area of camouflage is no exception.

The art of concealing oneself is a very wide subject, and one that is constantly changing. The different areas of the human body require different approaches and are governed by such considerations as freedom of movement, hearing, sight and comfort.

THE HEAD

The head is usually the only part of a sniper that is in line of sight to the enemy and so must be concealed to the highest standard. In doing so he must bear in mind that a sniper's senses of sight, sound and smell are three of his biggest weapons in the fight to survive on any battlefield. To that end the headwear must not impinge these senses in any way.

The choices of headwear are usually between a hood attached to the ghillie suit, or a separate hat such as the issued jungle or "boonie" hat. Whichever is chosen, and again it is personal choice, it must be constructed with the same amount of forethought and detail as the suit. The elastic must be applied in different planes, and the hessian must be carefully attached. The headwear must be "ghillied" enough to break up the distinctive human head shape but not to the point that it draws attention to itself. It should blend into the shoulder camouflage of the suit to destroy any hint of a human outline, but care must be taken to allow as much freedom of movement and unimpaired hearing as possible.

It is impossible to camouflage the head and shoulders and not reduce the level of hearing, and so a sensible compromise must be reached. This is achieved by trial and error in the construction phase. When the sniper is crawling around on his stomach his vision across the surrounding area is severely restricted and so his ears become his primary defence. He should never make the assumption that his headwear construction will allow good hearing, but always try it out. It may well work on a basic sniper course where he does not have a mobile enemy hunting him, but on operations it may not be up to the job. If the sniper opts for a hood attached to his suit he has the added thickness of the material to further restrict his hearing.

This can be overcome by cutting holes in the area of the ears and attaching pieces of face veil in the gaps. This permits better hearing and the face veil netting provides additional camouflage where the material has been cut away. Most snipers prefer a combination of the two – the jungle hat for the approach to a target or for general movement, and the attached hood for use in the final phase of a stalk or once in the final fire position. The attachment of netting to the inside of the hood, or the front of the hat is another popular option, which may also provide extra camouflage to the

ABOVE: A Slovenian sniper wearing his ghillie suit. The basic construction is fine, but he has over-done the hessian to the point where it will hinder movement. It is also in stark contrast to his backdrop.

BELOW: Two US tank drivers' cold weather face masks are shown to illustrate the huge difference that the application of hessian makes in helping to conceal the true shape of whatever it is attached to.

face, since camouflage cream is not always enough to conceal the shine of human skin.

If using a hat of any design the sniper would be wise to attach it to the ghillie suit in some way with para cord. This would prevent the loss of it at night if it is pushed off his head by vegetation, or by day if he is forced to move quickly due to enemy activity. The enemy should be unaware of a sniper's presence but, while he may not see the sniper, if he found a lost piece of his stalker's equipment it would awaken him to a threat in the area and hence increase his vigilance and efforts to destroy the sniper. Camouflage is not just a physical thing; it's a state of mind as well.

THE HANDS

The hands are another area of the sniper's body that are likely to give him away if not concealed with the same effort as the main torso. In fact, any of the sniper's extremities can lead to his discovery and death if not camouflaged correctly. The sniper's main adversary is another sniper and so he must work under the assumption that his enemy will be looking for any tiny exposures of human shape in order to locate him.

To this end the hands must be concealed and this is done with some form of glove. This is where sniping moves away from some of the recognised rulings of normal military teachings on shooting. In normal military circumstances soldiers are positively encouraged never to wear gloves while shooting, for fear of losing that all-important sense of touch between finger and trigger, and hence adversely affecting the smooth release of the shot. In sniping that is all different. The sniper *must* have some form of protection on

his hands because of the punishment they receive while moving across the battlefield. He must also have his hands concealed at all times from observation, and therefore the obvious answer is to wear a pair of gloves.

The selection and type of glove is up to the individual; what works for one may not work for another. This leads to a wide variety of gloves being used, from military issue to civilian shooting or gardening types, and each is usually modified in some way by the sniper. This can take the form of cutting one or more "fingers" off, to aid the trigger/finger relationship, or even the wearing of an entirely different glove on each hand. Whatever the choice the gloves must be "ghillied" and have elastic attached in exactly the same way as before.

The hands most also be covered in camouflage cream/paint even though the sniper is wearing gloves, since if the situation dictates that the sniper must remove his glove at some stage, then he cannot risk a bare human hand being exposed, even for a short time. This cream must be checked at regular intervals due to the effects of sweat removing it inside the glove, but care must be taken to ensure that the hands remain out of sight from the surrounding area at all times while the check is carried out.

The sniper must train in his selected glove at all times, whether it is during field craft or on-the-range shooting. He must get used to working in them and still be able to carry out his tasks whatever the situation or environment. If at any stage in his training he finds he cannot, then he must try again with another type until he finds a pair that he can operate in. It is not uncommon to find a sniper carrying more than one pair of gloves to suit the needs of the operation, but care must be exercised to avoid carrying too many options and ending up like a small glove store.

THE SKIN

The human skin is very easy to locate among natural vegetation due to its colour and shine. While it is true that some

BELOW: Note how this sniper's map stands out. It will draw attention from some considerable distance and so needs to be shielded from view by the sniper. Also note the way the hessian breaks up the general shape of the rifle across his lap: a painted rifle is still rifle-shaped!

different skin tones are easier to locate than others, in general untreated human flesh will give a sniper away. The military have long catered for this with camouflage cream for just about every type of terrain, from European woodland to desert. Each has it good and bad points, but as a whole they are very effective. Some contain insect repellent, others sun screen, and some are even made by well-known cosmetic make-up manufacturers! The main area of concern, however, is not its properties or who makes it, but how it is applied.

Every soldier has his own ideas on what pattern and application technique makes for the best concealment. Military manuals from around the world suggest how best to apply face and hand camouflage, giving pictorial examples of "too much, too little and just right". For the average soldier the aim is to achieve a break-up of the obvious human outline and skin tone by the use of coloured creams. For the sniper it is to achieve the complete deception and concealment of any human presence even under intense optical scrutiny. This requires a great deal more thought and knowledge of both nature and how to copy it. The sniper must apply the cream in such a way as to give his face depth so that it blends with his surroundings when under observation, and the main way to achieve this is to emulate the vegetation around him.

This would suggest that one method or application is not enough, and that is the case. The sniper must be prepared to modify or change the camouflage to his hands and face several times during a stalk. While static in an observation position (OP) the need to change is obviously reduced, although any changes in light or shadow will still have to be com-

ABOVE: A British sniper adjusts netting to conceal his optic from view. Note the minimal amount of hessian applied to the rifle and the green tape used to dull the remainder of it. When applied so that it does not interfere with the floating barrel this camouflage does not affect accuracy.

a   b   c

ABOVE: There is no point concealing body and rifle if the sniper neglects to conceal his face. He must be adept at the application of face camouflage, starting with a thin application to the whole face, neck and hands (a). He takes note of the direction of growth and predominant colour of surrounding foliage and marks his face to match (b). Finally, he adds depth and shading to break the human shape. Skilled application of white cream can help solve the problem of eyes.

pensated for. The sniper must acquire the skill of knowing what his position looks like from the enemy point of view and camouflage his face accordingly. This is also the principle for his entire position, but the face requires special attention, since it is the main area exposed to the enemy's gaze. The sniper can use a suitably ghillied-up facemask, such as the American cold weather tank driver's mask, but these, while suitable for static positions, are not suitable for movement due to the build-up of heat involved, and so the application of camouflage cream is important. To achieve success the sniper must be aware of the problems he will encounter and plan accordingly.

The famous "whites of their eyes" situation is another problem that the sniper must overcome. The most effective method used by successful World War II British snipers was to apply white camouflage cream in vertical or diagonal patterns across or around the eyes to break up the eye shape and to give the impression of sunlight breaking through foliage, or to use it on other areas of the face to take away attention from the eyes. Whatever method is adopted is up to the individual, but the sniper cannot simply ignore it and he cannot apply cream to the eyes, so trial and error during training will undoubtedly improve his chances of success and ultimately survival.

The effective application of camouflage to the face is another area that will only be perfected with training and practice. Nobody has a monopoly on good ideas; the speed at which the sniper masters it will depend upon his willingness to learn from others, plus good old-fashioned practice instead of the latest styling adopted by Hollywood!

THE FEET

Camouflaging the feet is an area that is all too often overlooked, and failure to do so effectively represents a very common way that snipers are caught on basic training courses, indicating the importance of correctly concealing this area of the body. Most armies issue their soldiers with black boots. This, as has previously discussed, is a colour

that has little or no equal in nature and so the reason behind the issue of such a colour to a fighting force is somewhat confusing. The reasoning must be related to cost or preferred appearance, since the issue of a tan or brown boot would greatly enhance the camouflage effect of the issued uniforms. The argument that is always put forward is that of, "Well, who is going to see your boots as they are always hidden by grass or undergrowth?" This may indeed apply to the average soldier, who rarely seems to crawl anywhere these days, but to the sniper the colour of his boots is a serious matter.

The sniper spends a great deal of time preparing himself before entering battle and the majority of that time is on his camouflage. To this end the neglect of his footwear would be a very dangerous oversight. To wear a ghillie suit and couple it with black boots indicates either a lack of experi-

BELOW: Too many snipers overlook their footwear and make the mistake of wearing black boots. This may seem pernickety, but the feet are level with the sniper's head for most of the time, and there is little black in nature. Camouflaged boots can be obtained, but soles should also be camouflaged!

ABOVE: A good example of how obvious black boots can be, even in a black and white picture! The sniper is well blended with his surroundings except for the two lumps of black that draw the eye to him. Some snipers have even been known to leave the price stickers on.

ence or a lack of dedication on the part of the sniper.

The concealment of the feet can be achieved in several different ways. Firstly there are some very good camouflaged boots to be found in civilian hunting supply shops and magazines, and these would more than satisfy the requirement. But here a word of warning: the majority of these boots, while superbly camouflaged on their uppers, are all fitted with *black* soles. On first reflection, this would not seem to be too much of a problem because, after all, the soles are on the floor. *Wrong*, because snipers are crawling, which means that for a good proportion of the time the soles of the boot will be visible, so a black sole is just as bad as a black boot!

With time and patience it is possible to find camouflaged boots that also have camouflaged soles. Alternatively, ghillie can be attached to a pair of issued boots to make them an extension of the suit, or the sniper can wear sandbags over his issue boots to conceal their colour, or a suitable civilian boot that is a less obtrusive colour can be found.

If the sniper attaches natural foliage to his footwear, he should be sure to fix it in such a way as to ensure that when he is moving, be it upright or crawling, the foliage points in the same natural direction that he is trying to emulate. There is nothing more obvious to a trained observer than badly applied vegetation, since it is a clear indication of the presence of man.

PERSONAL EQUIPMENT

Apart from his weapon, a sniper will always have to carry a certain amount of military kit on him while stalking. This will vary from operation to operation, but will include such items as spare ammunition, food, water, maps, optics or night vision goggles (NVGs), radios, compasses and all

manner of other things. To do this he will have to have made provision for it on his ghillie suit, and more than likely have to wear some form of webbing or belt kit. Again the choice is personal, and may indeed vary from task to task. The most common choices are a webbing belt with one or two issue pouches attached, or an issued chest rig usually worn backwards across the lower back so as to not hinder crawling. Both options however will need to be ghillied-up and have elastic attached as for all other forms of sniper equipment. This attention to detail covers all areas of the sniper's trade and is one of the main reasons he is better than the average soldier.

ABOVE: Basic sniper pair equipment – l to r, rucksack and webbing, night vision goggles and thermal sight, poles to aid hide construction, digging tool, warm kit, weapon night sights, SA80 assault and L96A1 sniper rifles, camouflage nets, thermal sheeting and ghillie suits.

BELOW: Sniper pair preparing for deployment via Land Rover.

Along with the load-carrying equipment there is also the need to camouflage any piece of kit that could be exposed to the enemy's gaze.

BINOCULARS

These also seem to only be issued in one colour, black, and this obviously needs to be addressed. They can be painted, or more likely have a green tape applied to their outer casing and then camouflaged using a combination of camouflage cream and face veil. A suitable green tape can be found in the issued nuclear, biological, chemical (NBC) repair tape such as that the British Army uses. Indeed, this tape is trea-

sured by the British sniper community, who liberally apply it to most of their kit as part of their concealment preparation. The other area on the binoculars that requires attention is the objective lens. The perfectly round shape of the objective lens on any optic will very quickly be spotted by a trained observer if not camouflaged. The reason for this is that, because animals have yet to perfect the art of digging perfectly circular holes, the only conclusion an observer could come to when he locates one is that it is a man-made object, and hence a soldier. To avoid this, the circular shape must be broken up. This can be achieved in different ways. One is to apply tape to the objective lens casing, being care-

ABOVE: A British sniper pair working very hard during training. They have adopted a very good position set deep back in the shadows of a tree line. However, they failed because the

observer picked out the prominent dark circle that was the sniper's telescopic lens. A simple piece of netting would have avoided this: snipers must pay attention to detail.

ABOVE: This sniper has attempted to conceal the circular lens with green tape. This is a workable option, but too straight a line can be as prominent as the circular lens.

BELOW: By contrast, this sniper has draped a piece of netting over the rifle scope. Even close up it can be seen how effective it is in breaking the line of the lens.

ful not to stick any on the lens itself, and then cut out enough to allow good vision through the optic, while concealing the true shape of the lens. Another is to attach face veil over both lenses; while the sniper will still be able to see through the optic, the circular shape will be hidden. Some amount of ghillie can also be applied but care must be exercised to avoid impairing the free function of the optic's focus and clarity.

TELESCOPE

Most snipers are issued some form of spotting scope, usually a tripod-mounted telescope, for detailed observation and for the correction of the fall of shot over extreme ranges. This too must be subjected to the attentions of camouflage skills. A fairly common practice is to either paint it or to apply the British-issue type green tape and hessian. The tripod must also receive the same attention. Care must again be exercised to avoid impairing any of the telescope's functions or clarity.

THE RIFLE

Here lies an area of controversy. There is a train of thought within the sniper community that to apply any form of camouflage, other than paint, would degrade the weapon's performance. While I would agree that any hessian or other type of camouflage that interfered with the barrel action on a fully floating barrel would indeed affect the weapon's overall accuracy, I would not agree that a single layer of hessian applied to the barrel, with care to avoid impairing the barrel's movement, would affect the weapon. Indeed, I cannot see how the weapon and hence the sniper can remain concealed when the barrel is not camouflaged in any way except with paint. A camouflage-painted rifle barrel is still

ABOVE: A French sniper keeps low and blends with the colours of the lower vegetation. Standing, he would become very prominent against the very dark green to his rear.

BELOW: A Gurkha pair use the dead ground of the river and noise of the water to cover their movement, the sniper at low left covering his partner's movements.

rifle-shaped and will be located by another sniper or well-trained observer. The other often-quoted reason for not applying hessian to the weapon barrel is that when wet the extra weight will cause the rifle to lose accuracy. I have yet to see any evidence of this and indeed have tried such hessian-wrapped rifles on the range, with no noticeable change in either accuracy or point of impact in relation to the point of aim. With the main defence of a sniper being his ability to remain unseen, I think I would happily accept the miniscule changes in accuracy, if there were any, and remain undetected, rather than risk being seen and more than likely killed because my barrel was not camouflaged.

APPLICATION OF NATURAL CAMOUFLAGE

The basic elements of applying foliage to oneself are taught to all military recruits in the early stages of their training. In the ideal world they would remember and apply that knowledge throughout their careers, but this rarely happens. The truth is that in most armies the basic skill of camouflage has been allowed to slip, and this has led to the sniper having an even greater advantage over his enemy. The sniper uses all the common infantry skills, but takes them a stage further than the average soldier and is best summed up in the British Army description of sniping: "Sniping is the basic art of infantry soldiering taken to such a level that it has become specialist."

The application of foliage to oneself would appear to be fairly straightforward, with the main aim being to look like one's surroundings. However, the sniper knows that to be convincing requires a detailed study of the area in which he is to work. The potential sniper within the British system will spend several lessons in a classroom being taught about the theory of camouflage and concealment before he is taken into the field to practise. In this way it is hoped to avoid the all too common mistakes that sniper instructors

ABOVE: There are four snipers concealed in this photo during a training session, a good example of snipers' ability to "vanish", primarily due to the ghillie suit breaking up the human shape.

BELOW: A sniper uses natural vegetation attached to his ghillie suit combined with a good, low-level position in a dip to "disappear" in his surroundings and against his backdrop.

the world over experience. A sniper is taught that it is not enough to simply stick grass in the headdress and ghillie suit – the grass must look and react in the same way as its surroundings.

A common mistake is to pull up grass up and stick it in the headdress, roots and all! I have yet to see grass growing with its roots above the ground, so when another sniper spots this through his optics, it tells him that someone has applied camouflage to himself, badly, and hence draws the sniper's attention.

The sniper must change his camouflage each time he moves through a different type of cover. This is time-consuming but when it is considered that the sniper pair is usually away from friendly support and more often than not behind enemy lines, to fail to take the time to do this could lead to an early grave.

DIFFERENT THEATRES OF OPERATION

Most of the rules and knowledge discussed above apply to general war. There is, however, a role for snipers in all phases of conflict and in all areas of the world. The sniper must be prepared to deploy in any area of the world and con-

ceal himself once on the ground. This would obviously lead to changes in the way he operates and the way he would camouflage himself. Overall, the main techniques of the sniper's trade change very little, with the exception of his camouflage.

DESERT

The sniper is ideally suited to desert warfare. The vast open areas allow the sniper to use his shooting skills and his ability to remain unseen to the full. The Coalition forces in the Kuwaiti desert superbly demonstrated this during Operation Desert Storm, where both British and American forces deployed and used snipers. The desert in many areas is not the rolling sand dunes of one's imagination, but vast areas of craggy uneven wasteland where a suitably coloured ghillie suit was found to work just as well as it does in the green areas of Europe. The main difference was the reduced layering of hessian to compensate for the extremely high temperatures. The compromise that had to be sought was that of clothing that was strong enough to take the harsh desert environment and yet airy enough to allow circulation and avoid the threat of heat-related injuries or illness.

USE OF COVER

The sniper must have an above average ability to read the ground and identify areas and routes that will give him cover from the enemy and the ground that will enable him to dominate a larger force or area of land. Without the correct use of cover, a sniper's ability to conceal himself could be wasted. It stands to reason therefore that to make the most of his skills the sniper must develop a high level of forethought and imagination in the planning and execution of his mission. To do this the sniper follows the following guidelines:

- Always try to blend with the background from the enemy's viewpoint and where possible travel with a suitable screen and backdrop to increase the chances of going unnoticed.
- Never break skylines or become silhouetted against natural straight lines. This draws the attention of the eye and could lead to the sniper being located and engaged.
- Avoid any isolated cover. Not only is this difficult to move to or from, but its isolation will naturally draw the enemy's attention.
- Regularly check and where necessary change or add to natural camouflage. Lack of attention to detail in this area will almost certainly lead to the sniper being compromised and probably killed.
- When working in soft cover, always observe and where necessary shoot through the cover. Appearing above the cover is unnecessary exposure to the enemy's gaze and totally unprofessional.
- Try to use natural or trapped shadow to conceal movement. Remember that powerful optics can penetrate limited shadow so the sniper must not assume he is invisible and therefore take short-cuts. Also, remember that the sun moves and hence so do the shadows, so the sniper must remain aware of his position in relation to the shadow and how its movement will affect his own.
- Avoid any unnecessary or quick movement, since both catch the eye. Always try to move under cover and plan the route to minimise exposure.

Above: A British sniper in the Kuwaiti desert using a combination of his colour and surroundings to aid his concealment. If used correctly the ghillie suit will work just as well here as in a more general theatre of operations.

Jungle

The jungle is not the best area to maximise the many skills of the sniper, but he can still be used to devastating effect, as the Japanese proved during the island campaigns in the Pacific in World War II. The abundance of close, dense vegetation coupled to the heat mean that the ghillie suit is not essential but in static positions will still aid the sniper in remaining undetected, even when the enemy is at close range. This was recently demonstrated by the British Special Air Service who, in a recent rescue of captured troops from the "West Side Boys" in Sierra Leone, used ghillie suits to aid the concealment of their OP party located within 110 yards (100m) of the rebel camp. They remained undetected for five days, revealing themselves only when they opened fire on the rebels to cover the arrival of the rescue party. While this was not directly sniping, it does illustrate the effect of the ghillie suit in jungle conditions.

Arctic

Again, the vast open areas associated with snow-covered regions lend themselves quite nicely to sniping. The obvious difference is that the ghillie suit is of no practical use except

Below: A British sniper undergoing training in Arctic conditions, using a white camouflage net to aid his concealment. The application of tape and light sheeting material can also effectively hide the rifle.

ABOVE: Dead ground exists in Arctic regions as well, and should always be taken advantage of. Here a British sniper moves steadily across open ground, although it would have been better to move along to his left side where his shadow would have blended with that of the ground and aided in his concealment: never forget the sun's location!

in the lower regions or among rocky areas. The primary camouflage used by the sniper in this environment is the issued snow over-suit. There are many varied versions of the snowsuit, from the British lightweight all-white to the German heavier white-and-green tree-line pattern. The civilian market is also awash with different snow suits based on various camouflage patterns. Whichever is chosen it is worth noting that snow varies in whiteness from pure white high up, to a dirty white lower down where it is subject to more grime.

Camouflage should mirror the snow in the area in which the sniper has to operate. His kit should also be suitably camouflaged with white material or tape, applying the same level of detail as he would in any other area. The weapon must also be camouflaged with either white paint or a combination of tape and material. Care must be given to avoid using anything that could freeze and impair the operational effectiveness of either the weapon or the equipment.

URBAN

The prospect of deploying into an urban area is one that grows more likely every day. In fact, British snipers have been working in such areas in Northern Ireland for over twenty years. The problems with camouflage in the urban area vary, dependent upon the scale of the conflict and the type of enemy the sniper is up against. These fall into two main categories; all-out war and operations other than war.

The effects that all-out war will have on the urban environment will require a completely different approach to concealment. Camouflage patterns are all based on disruptive patterns and the fact that nature has very few straight lines. The urban environment is a man-made one, and there is very little "nature" to be seen there, and so the rules are all different.

During recent years there has been an increasing number of so-called "urban camouflage" suits appearing on the market. All of these suits are based on the normal "green" camouflage patterns but with the greens and browns changed to greys and blacks. While these suits are very snazzy to look at, they are all but useless in practical camouflage terms. The reason for this would appear to be obvious: the urban area is made up almost entirely of straight lines, so a suit based on disruptive patterns does not work. The most effective urban camouflage I have seen is that applied to British Army vehicles in the old Berlin Brigade in the 1980s and which I used as a basis for a very successful sniper suit in recent years.

If a city has been subjected to any form of bombardment the resulting damage will just add to the straight lines, and therefore the only way to effectively disappear and yet still be able to move around is going to be in a suit based on a straight-line design. The colours of any suit will still depend on the predominant colours within the city and will not necessarily be grey and black. The attention to detail that the sniper applies to preparing for the "green" deployment must also be applied to the urban environment. This includes his normal equipment and weapon, and also the fact that he may need to carry kit not normally needed, such as ropes and a crow bar. The urban area is one that is fraught with danger but it is a sniper's playground. A careful and professional sniper will be very hard to remove.

ABOVE: Urban combat has its own set of rules. Here a British sniper uses the author's urban design camouflage and suit; it may appear to be "load" but works in situ when the author's principles of construction are applied.

BELOW: Here the sniper makes no physical attempt to conceal himself, merely standing against a house wall wearing the author's urban suit. The fragmented nature of the pattern minimises the need for him to hide behind objects.

CONSTRUCTION AND USE OF HIDES

The use of camouflaged or concealed positions has always been the basis of the sniper's trade. This is more usually assumed to be the concealment of the individual by means of clothing and natural vegetation, but in different phases of combat the basic tactic can be taken much further. This elevation of the skill usually applies when the sniper or sniper pair are going to be used to watch over an enemy position and report back to friendly forces, and therefore will need to remain static and concealed for a considerable time, or if they are to be used in a defensive role where the task is to ambush or delay an enemy's advance. In either situation the sniper will need some form of forward-mounting base from which to work, and this is known as a hide or observation position (OP).

ADVANTAGES OF HIDES

- Allows the sniper a certain amount of freedom of movement to observe and shoot.
- Makes locating the sniper and eliminating him all but impossible.
- Affords the sniper all-round cover from enemy view and fire.
- Provides the sniper with limited protection from the elements.
- Allows the sniper to remain offensively operational for longer periods.

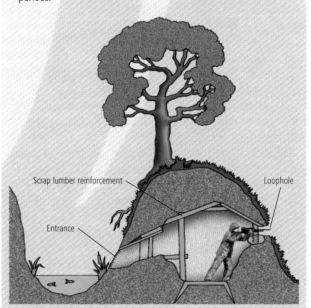

Scrap lumber reinforcement   Loophole

Entrance

DISADVANTAGES OF HIDES

- Correct siting and camouflage very time-consuming.
- Difficult to enter or leave unless covered approaches are available.
- Limits sniper's mobility.
- Construction is time-consuming and noisy, and can be manpower-intensive.

CONSIDERATIONS IN HIDE SELECTION

- The type of operation the sniper is employed on.
- The overall battlefield situation and desired results of the deployment.
- The specific and implied tasks given to the sniper.
- The time factor.
- The type of terrain to be deployed into.
- The enemy's intentions and expected reactions.
- The enemy's standard operating procedures (SOPs).

There are several different types of hide, each one with its own advantages and disadvantages, and the tactical situation and terrain will dictate which is the most suitable for the sniper's task. A dictionary definition of a hide is: "Put, keep out of sight, conceal, keep secret; conceal oneself; place of concealment, e.g.: for bird watcher."

The relevance of a hide to the sniper can readily understood, and how with a more static base, he will be effective for longer. The exact choice of hide type will be affected by a number of factors and considerations, and these will determine how hasty or elaborate the hide will be. In offensive operations, where snipers may be deployed ahead of the main force in order to locate and report an enemy, they may well select an area from which to operate and then, if time dictates, construct a hide to increase their chances of remaining undetected.

In the internal security role, such as in Northern Ireland, the snipers' ability to move into close proximity to the enemy and remain unseen provides an excellent intelligence-gathering asset, and as well as being able to establish a pattern-of-life study from their OP, the snipers can also provide a counter-sniper option for the protection of more overt troops.

In the defensive role the hides can be sited to cover vulnerable points such as gaps in defences, bridges, river crossing points and likely enemy approach routes. The advantages of hides are obvious but unless care is taken in their siting and camouflage, the whole concept is flawed.

PLANNING

For the hide to work a great deal of attention to detail must be adopted in the planning phase. The driving force will be the results it is wished to achieve, and an in-depth map ground and air photo study must be carried out to initially locate the desired OP location. If time permits, a recce of the site should also take place, but this is rare except in defensive operations. When the hide construction begins

ABOVE: In the urban or anti-terrorist scenario, snipers can be deployed so that they get very close to a target and remain unseen while reporting on the target's movements, moving from passive to active engagement when ordered.

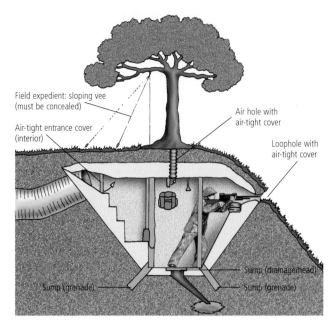

Field expedient: sloping vee (must be concealed)

Air-tight entrance cover (interior)

Air hole with air-tight cover

Loophole with air-tight cover

Sump (drainage/head)

Sump (grenade)

Sump (grenade)

ABOVE: In long-term defence or anti-terrorist operations a semi-permanent or deep hide location can be constructed with snipers being relieved by other sniper teams at regular intervals to facilitate long-term operations.

care must be taken not to disturb the surrounding area too much, since this ground sign will act like an aiming mark to the enemy. A strict track plan must be enforced and any spoil from the construction must be expertly camouflaged itself to avoid drawing the enemy's attention to the area. The OP must be made to look exactly the same as the surrounding area once complete, and the observation aperture must be equally well concealed.

HIDE PLANNING CONSIDERATIONS

- Routes in and out of the hide, and escape routes.
- Construction materials needed and how to get them there.
- The equipment needed.
- The likely duration of the operation.
- Resupply if needed.
- Communication and communications failure drill.
- Thermal threat.
- Manpower and routine.
- Compromise drill.

LIKELY HIDE LOCATIONS

- Cuttings.
- Hedgerows and bushes.
- Banks or mounds.
- Riverbanks.
- Wood lines.
- Buildings.
- Vehicles.
- Anywhere else that can be found.

TYPES OF HIDE

ENLARGED FIRE TRENCH: This is a modification of the standard infantry fire trench but with far superior camouflage.

ADVANTAGES	DISADVANTAGES
• Low silhouette.	• Restricted access during daylight.
• Two-man position.	• Limited cover from enemy view and fire.
• The size means that it can be occupied for longer periods.	

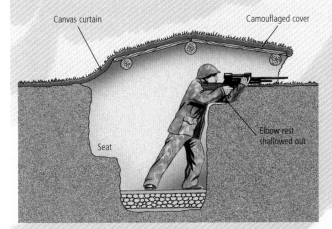

BELLY HIDE: Used in a fairly fluid situation, such as the withdrawal, when time is not necessarily on the sniper's side.

ADVANTAGES	DISADVANTAGES
• Simple and quick.	• Uncomfortable, cannot be occupied for long.
• Gives a low silhouette.	• Limited cover from enemy view and fire.

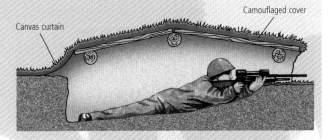

SEMI-PERMANENT: This is the true sub-surface hide and the one that with careful concealment and siting will remain undetected for a long time.

ADVANTAGES	DISADVANTAGES
• Extended occupation with relief in place an option.	• Very time- and manpower-intensive during construction.
• Gives good cover from enemy view and fire.	• Stores needed for construction.
• Allows for an element of comfort and routine.	• High risks of ground sign in surrounding area.
• If not located by the enemy, can be used again.	

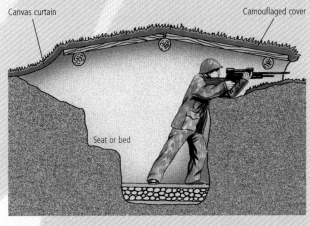

BUSHES

One of the most commonly used hides is the bush. This is not only because of the bountiful selection on most pieces of land, but mainly because it takes very little time to construct and requires few materials. The selection of the site takes as much thought as any other location, with all the considerations that go with it. The bush must be tactically sited and offer a high chance of success to the sniper pair, as well as a concealed escape route. The bush must not be isolated and have enough depth and trapped shadow to conceal the sniper pair.

Once the selection has been made the pair decide an entry point on the opposite side to the enemy. One man carries out the construction while the other acts as local pro-

tection. The construction should be carried out with minimum noise and with minimum disturbance to the bush. To this end the pair do not cut the bush unless they have to, preferring to fold back or tie back the internal branches in order to make the working space or hide. It must be remembered that any string, etc., must be removed when the snipers leave so as to not provide any indication that they were there and thereby give away an operational tactic. Once the hide/OP has been constructed the security man can move into the hide with the construction man to reduce the risk of compromise from a passing enemy patrol.

The pair can set about the camouflage of the position. First, a false "door" must be made to cover the entry point,

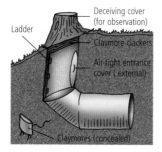

Deceiving cover
(for observation)

Ladder

Claymore clackers

Air-tight entrance
cover (external)

Claymores (concealed)

LEFT: The entrance to a hide must be cleverly concealed to protect the sniper's location. Defensive measures such as ground sensors or anti-personnel devices will be employed to assist the sniper's extraction if he is aggressively compromised.

and is usually constructed over a section of wire mesh that the pair will have brought along. The crawl tunnel that runs from the entry point to the main hide will have at least one right angle turn in its length. This will ensure that if any passing enemy patrol should look into the bush as they go by they do not look straight into the hide, but will see only as far as the bend and hence see only a gap in a bush.

The enemy side, the side from which snipers will observe and possibly shoot, will have a small one-man personnel camouflage net set up between the pair and the inside of the bush as an added protection against discovery from probing enemy optics. This will give added depth and assist in retaining trapped shadow, irrespective of the movements of the sun or changing light conditions. To the outside world it is a very dense bush, but inside it is an observation station, an administration position and an entry tunnel containing a very deadly secret.

URBAN HIDE

The urban hide is governed by all the same criteria as the rural ones but offers the sniper pair the most comfortable position in terms of freedom of movement and protection from enemy view and fire. The pair must first site themselves in such a way as to cover their allotted task. The provision of a proved and rehearsed escape route is essential if the pair is to survive. The urban environment is a very dan-

ABOVE: For specialised operations there are several options regarding clothing. Illustrated here are three of the options available, but there are many more both issued and on the civilian hunter market. Left to right: US desert night camouflage, author's patented urban camouflage, and the entry team black.

BELOW: Here the sniper, wearing the author's urban camouflage design, has laid himself among the rubble of the building but has made little physical attempt at concealment. Even after it has been battle-damaged the urban arena will remains a mass of straight lines, with only the colours varying.

gerous one that can change very quickly, and if the snipers are not on their guard they can quickly fall to the enemy advance.

Buildings offer a multitude of options to the sniper, from attics to space under the floorboards, but whichever he chooses he must avoid the temptation to get too close to the window or chosen aperture in order to improve his arc of view and fire. To do this would be to tempt fate, and greatly increase the chances of discovery. In an urban situation the sniper must accept that his arcs are going to be greatly decreased. To compensate for this he must carefully site his position in order to inflict as much hurt on the enemy as he can, by covering an area the enemy must advance through or one that is his expected line of advance.

The key to a successful urban hide is in staying back in the shadows and, with cunning construction, to conceal the sniper's position. When he sites his hide in a room he must first of all never choose a ground floor one, since this would greatly increase the risk of accidental discovery by a passing person who just happens to just look through the window, which is the normal human reaction. So the sniper must go higher, but avoid going too high.

Once the hide is selected, a false wall, or drop, can be constructed using any suitable material and colouring it to match the room walls. This can be attached to the walls and ceiling in any way possible, but it must not be obvious from the outside. Then the sniper pair can build up a solid observation and shooting position from any available furniture

FACTORS AFFECTING THE POSITION OF AN URBAN HIDE

- Mission.
- Type of urban environment.
- Type of building, protection, routes in and out, entry/exit points, escape routes, construction required, natural apertures, lighting/noise, shadow.
- Distance from OP to target, time of year, weather, light, smoke/smog, heat haze.
- Resources, manpower needed, split OP, insertion/extraction teams, transport, equipment, communications.
- Compromise risk.
- Local pattern of life, social activities, traffic/pedestrians, children's play areas.

HIDE OCCUPATION SEQUENCE OF EVENTS

- Preparation and planning.
- Day and night reconnaissance.
- Orders and rehearsals.
- Insertion.
- Gaining entry.
- Occupation/construction.
- Routine.
- Resupply/relief in place.
- Extraction.
- De-briefing.

TYPES OF URBAN ENVIRONMENT

OLD TOWN

- Less open.
- Back-to-back terraced houses with walled yards and alleyways.
- Some derelict and empty houses.
- Areas of waste land.
- Lighting often poor.
- Dense population in smaller areas, likely to be "rougher" than on a new estate.

NEW TOWN

- More open.
- Fewer alleyways.
- Population tend to notice movement within the area.
- Construction sites.

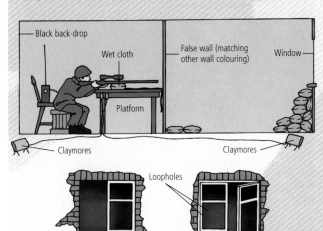

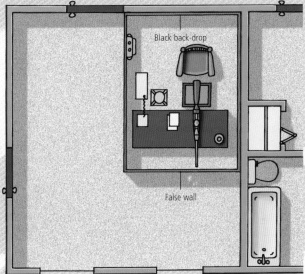

behind the false wall, and make a small vision port in the false wall material to allow observation. Behind their position the pair can put up a dark-coloured drop to ensure that any available outside light does not silhouette them against their false wall and thereby compromise them.

If time is short then the darkness of the attic or cellar will offer adequate hide positions, but the snipers must still stay back in the room and also avoid the obvious "Hollywood" bell tower position. Snipers must avoid the roof if possible since it is very difficult to locate a firing and observation position without looking over an edge, which would break one of the main rules of concealment – that of not looking over cover and risking being sky-lined. The roof is a very poor option for a sniper, although it is often used by police marksmen, who rarely have to worry about return fire let alone retaliatory indirect artillery fire!

THERMAL CAMOUFLAGE

When thermal sights and observation devices were introduced to the battlefield, it was predicted that this would be the end of snipers. Not so. The sniper must keep abreast of any invention or technological advance that will threaten his ability to operate, and such was the case with thermal imaging. The thermal sight works on the principle of taking the

heat given off by, or reflected from the sun's rays on, any given object, be it human, animal, vegetation or inanimate object, and transferring this heat into a moving image. In principle, this would appear to make remaining hidden from view very difficult if not impossible. But with every man-made object there is a disadvantage or weakness, and snipers are by nature cunning, so it was not too long before they found a way around this problem.

Thermal imagers reflect what they can see, and so the most obvious answer is to not be seen! This can be achieved using methods of movement that are a way of life to a sniper. Snipers are taught to always plan their route to maximise the available cover route across the battlefield – that is, out of direct line of sight to the enemy. If the sniper is out of direct line of sight due to a bank, ditch or heavy vegetation, then thermal imagers cannot see him. The easiest and most effective way to defeat thermal imagers is to remain in

BELOW LEFT TO RIGHT: Today, thermal signature is a constant worry and industry is working very hard to come up with a suit to conceal a man's heat picture. These photos show several different approaches, all of which are very interesting to the sniper, both for his own protection and also for him to know how to defeat an enemy wearing one.

ground that is "dead" to them. A good knowledge of your enemy's equipment and standing operating procedures (SOPs) will enable the sniper to determine if his opponent has thermal optics and plan his route to avoid them.

If the intelligence about the enemy's likelihood of having thermal imagers is not available, or the sniper will have to breech open ground, then he can still do so under the scrutiny of thermal optics and remain unseen. This can be achieved in two ways. First, we know that thermal imagers work from the heat given off a given object, and that vegetation gives off a high signature. The sniper is already well versed in the use of natural vegetation to conceal himself and his equipment, and so, with the liberal application of natural camouflage that matches the vegetation he is to move across, he can remain unseen since his own "signature" will be masked by the heat given off by the natural foliage attached to him.

A modification to this method is the tried and tested concealment trick used by German snipers during World War II. They would use a normal umbrella or a constructed version and, by careful application of natural foliage to the front of it, conceal themselves from view by lying down behind it, and therefore out of sight. They would then slowly push out the umbrella to arm's length and move forward, repeating

the sequence, and in this way move unseen. To defeat thermal imagers in this way is easy since the imagers would see only the front of the umbrella and not what's behind it, with the signature of the natural foliage acting as a screen to shield the sniper.

Both of these methods are effective against thermal imagers and, while they are unlikely to mask the whole of a sniper's signature, they will reduce it to the level where any thermal operator ignores him, or believes him to be a small animal.

While snipers have been developing their own ways of defeating thermal imagers, the world's scientific minds are also working to develop methods of shielding against thermal discovery. One of the results is the use of sheets of material that work in conjunction with camouflage netting, but these are too big and cumbersome for the sniper. To overcome this the development of thermal-reflective suits is now actively being pursued by many nations for use by the likes of special forces, reconnaissance troops and, of course, snipers. This avenue of research will obviously be of interest to the sniper community, but until the scientists have perfected such a suit the sniper will keep on doing what he does best, defeating the enemy with professionalism and cunning.

SHOOTING TECHNIQUES

Sniping conjures up an image of a man firing a scoped rifle at a target some considerable distance away, and the act of shooting someone is considered to encompass the art of sniping. While it is essential to be able to engage enemy targets over great distances, there is no point in being able to hit targets if the sniper is seen before he takes his shot. It is evident therefore that sniping is a combination of several skills and not just shooting, although shooting is the easiest part of training to be a sniper, and for this reason it is usually the first phase of most sniper courses. If recruits cannot shoot, there is no point in wasting time and resources trying to get them through such areas as camouflage and concealment. Hesketh Pritchard's belief that anyone can be trained to be a good shot with a scoped rifle, is not necessarily true.

Over the course of his mission the sniper will be required to move through various types of foliage and cover, and may be called upon to take a shot at any time, so must be able to adopt a fire position wherever he is. To allow for this, the sniper is not only taught and well versed in all the normal shooting positions, but a number of "unconventional" ones as well. While the traditional teaching on shooting claims that to deviate from the recognised positions will lead to missing the target, the sniper is taught that as long as he applies the four basic marksmanship principles, and at the moment of shot release the cross hairs are on the target, he will hit home, no matter how awkward the position may look.

The man selected to attend a basic sniper course should have already shown an aptitude for shooting and ideally have achieved marksman status. This is not always the case

MARKSMANSHIP PRINCIPLES

- The position and hold must be firm enough to support the weapon.
- The weapon must point naturally at the target without any undue effort.
- The sight alignment must be correct.
- The shot must be released and followed through without disturbance to the position.

BELOW: A British sniper pair on a field firing range working with the Barrett .50 rifle. This weapon is an extremely cheap method of destroying very expensive pieces of military equipment, and when combined with the outstanding Leica laser range finders it is highly effective.

ABOVE: British and other NATO snipers engaging targets of unknown distance during a combined training exercise on Salisbury Plain, southern England.

Note how the painted but not camouflaged rifle nearest the camera stands out when compared to the hessian-covered weapons on the line.

and the start standard sometimes leaves a lot to be desired, with instructors struggling to raise the standard, often in a limited time frame. For this reason a lot of students fail at this early stage, all because they were wrongly put forward for a sniper course by a platoon commander who probably did not understand the standards required and did not ask.

However, sniper students would all have been trained in the recognised shooting positions and have a basic level of shooting experience using their army's issued infantry rifle. This will assist the instructors in raising the standard of shooting up to the required level of the sniper. The sniper students will then go through a programmed course of instruction covering weapon handling, shooting techniques, shooting positions and ballistics, culminating in the sniper qualification shoot.

WEAPON HANDLING

Each sniper student must be fully conversant with the sniper weapon of his military's choice and must be able to deploy or move around barracks with it in a safe manner. For many of the students it will be the first time that they have worked with a bolt-action or adjustable triggered rifle.

The student will be taught the weapon from the basics upwards, covering not only safe handling but also such areas as stripping and assembly, loading and unloading, the telescopic sight and the use of the rifle sling. The course will then progress to teaching the student how to zero his own personal weapon and how to adjust it to make the rifle his own personal fit, although they will also be taught how to compensate for the use of a weapon that is set up for someone else, such as his partner.

The sniper will be taught the smooth operation of the weapon's bolt and to avoid rapid arm movements when chambering a round, unless engaging multiple targets and using the rapid bolt manipulation technique that will also be taught. The student will be learn that for dedicated sniper work the bolt-action rifle is still the preferred choice of most professional snipers since the bolt gun is easier to control and hence quicker in re-acquiring any secondary targets when compared to the semi-automatic rifle. That is not to say that semi-automatic weapons are any less effective, but they are slower when engaging multiple targets compared to the bolt gun. The US Marines have a very effective demonstration of this on their advanced sniper course run at Quantico during the rapid bolt manipulation phase.

SHOOTING POSITIONS

The sniper must be fully conversant with many firing positions so that he has the maximum number of options while deployed on operations. While some positions may seem awkward or appear to break every rule on shooting, if the sniper can consistently hit the target, the instructor should leave the student alone.

THE PRONE OR LYING POSITION

This without doubt one of the steadiest firing positions and wherever possible the sniper will adopt it or a modified version of it. Its inherent stability comes from a combination of using the ground to support most of the weapon's weight and providing a high degree of comfort for the sniper. This position will also allow the sniper to present the lowest profile of himself towards the enemy and hence improve his chances of remaining undetected.

Before firing the sniper will go through a mental check list in his head to ensure his position is correct and that he has considered all the elements that combine to make for a steady shooting position:

- **THE BODY:** The body should be comfortable and lying slightly left of the line of fire (right for left-handed firing).
- **ELBOWS:** The elbows should always be a comfortable distance apart and this will vary from firer to firer. If the elbows are either too close or too far apart it will cause instability and lead to a lowering of overall shooting standards.
- **RIFLE SUPPORT:** The rifle must be supported by a combination of hands, the shoulder and the chin. The weapon must be pulled back into the chin in order to support the weapon, but over-stressing is to be avoided

since this will lead to too much tension in the firer and a degradation of his ability to point the weapon naturally towards the target.
- **FIRING HAND:** The firing hand is the primary supporting hand and the grip with it should be firm enough to support the weapon while avoiding over-grip, since this will lead to tension or strain and hence an unsteadiness and fatigue.
- **NON-FIRING HAND:** This hand acts as a support for the weapon's butt or the fore-stock, depending upon whether the bipod weapon support is used or not. This hand is usually placed against the chest and clenched into a fist to support the butt. By keeping the fist in contact with the butt the sniper can raise or lower the position of the weapon by clenching or relaxing his fist.
- **STOCK-WELD:** This is the instinctive ability of the sniper always to place his cheek on the same point on the stock each time he adopts a fire position. This aids stability and comfort of the position and is something that is gained with practice and experience. It also ensures that the sniper has the correct eye relief relative to the telescopic sight.
- **BONE SUPPORT:** The body supplies the sniper with the perfect framework to support his rifle, and is the foundation of the firing position.
- **MUSCLE RELAXATION:** The purpose of using the bone framework to support the weapon is to allow the sniper to relax muscle, thereby reducing unwanted movement caused by tense muscles. Any use of the muscles is going to generate movement in the sniper's position, hence the need for the position to be as comfortable as possible and thereby aid shooting performance.
- **TEST AND ADJUSTMENT:** The good shot will always test his position to ensure that the rifle points naturally towards the target. The way to ensure this is to adopt

BELOW: The prone bipod position is the most commonly used sniper-firing position, and offers the sniper a very stable and low shooting platform. (The rifle, as well as the soldier, would normally be camouflaged in the field.)

the fire position to be used and then close the eyes and take a few deep breaths. Upon opening the eyes the weapon's crosshairs should still be firmly across the intended target. If they are not, the body is not pointing naturally at the target and the position needs to be adjusted. The rifle is merely an extension of the sniper and by moving his body he will correct any faults in his position.

- **PRACTICE:** In order for the sniper to become proficient he must spend a great deal of time at practice. This covers not only live firing but also dry training, where the sniper will go through the process of adopting a position and releasing the shot without actually firing a live round. This drill applies to all firing positions and should not be under-estimated in its importance in sniper training.

THE HAWKINS POSITION

This position is a modification of the basic prone firing position and offers the sniper a lower profile than with the normal prone or lying position. It is used when firing from low cover or folds in the ground and is a very steady firing platform, offering the sniper both stability and concealment. To adopt the Hawkins position the following modifications must be made to the basic prone position:

- **THE BODY:** The body is positioned much more to the left/right of the weapon than is usual. This can even become almost a right angle to the line of the weapon.
- **NON-FIRING ARM:** This rests on the ground for the greater part of its length, with the hand holding the rifle by clenching a fist around the forward sling swivel. This

ABOVE: The Hawkins position places the full weight of the rifle on the ground, lowering the sniper's profile and reducing the likelihood of him being seen.

BELOW: The low profile offered by the Hawkins allows the sniper to adopt fire positions in vegetation too low to conceal a man.

means that the weapon is resting directly on top of the clenched fist.

- **THE BUTT:** The toe of the weapon butt should be resting on the ground, with the ground taking the full weight of the rifle and the butt tucked under the sniper's shoulder.
- **RECOIL:** By using the non-firing arm to maintain a forward pressure the rifles recoil can effectively be controlled. The weapon should not be placed butt first against anything solid as this may lead to damage to the rifle.

THE MODIFIED HAWKINS

When on soft ground or when on certain types of slope, achieving the correct muzzle depression may be difficult. In this instance the butt of the weapon can be placed into the point of the shoulder or the upper arm. Also when using a weapon with a pistol grip, such as the French FRF2, it may be necessary to dig in the pistol grip or to find a suitable depression in the ground in order to adopt the correct position.

THE LAID BACK POSITION

The laid back position has been used for many years and was indeed a popular position with the early musketeers. It has been the sniper with his reliance upon traditional methods that has kept this very steady shooting position alive. The laid back position is of particular use when firing down slopes and when the sniper wishes to achieve a high degree of accuracy combined with an unconventional appearance:

- **THE BODY:** The sniper should lay on his side with his legs together to provide support for the rifle. The legs also provide the ability to raise or lower the point of aim by simply opening or closing the leg position. The weapon butt should be in the shoulder and the non-firing hand should grasp the rifle in on overhand grip to provide stability.
- **EYE RELIEF:** With this position the eye relief is much greater than normal, and gives the sniper only a small floating aperture. It takes practice to centre this reduced sight picture, but as long as the head is steady it is achievable. It is also advisable to rest or support the head on available cover or on a piece of equipment such as a rucksack.

BELOW AND RIGHT: The laid back position offers the sniper an unusual profile to the observer and also a very stable shooting platform. The eye relief is greatly changed and this takes much practice, but once mastered it soon becomes habit.

OTHER FIRE POSITIONS

Fire positions that are used with other weapons can also be used when firing the sniper rifle. However, some will need modification to compensate for the change in centre of balance associated with the extra length of the sniper rifle when compared to today's assault weapons.

THE SITTING POSITION

This position can be adopted in several different ways, each one a slight modification of the other.

- **SITTING OPEN-LEGGED:** With this method the legs are kept a comfortable distance apart and the elbows are locked on the inside of the knees as low as possible. The body weight is allowed to relax forward, and the marksmanship principles are applied.
- **SITTING CROSS-LEGGED:** Exactly the same as the above with the exception of the legs being crossed at the ankles. The elbows can be rested either on the inside or the outside of the knees, whichever provides the firer with the most stable and comfortable position.

ABOVE: A sniper adopts the basic sitting position, with legs apart and elbows inside the knees to support the rifle.

- **SITTING ALTERNATIVE:** Both of the above positions can be modified to suit the individual. The main variation is in the hold and support of the rifle. The variation can be as simple as bending the non-firing arm at the elbow so that the rifle rests along the top of the arm and the forearm rests on top of the knee. The other and more extreme variation is where the shin bone is used to support the weapon by the sniper wrapping his non-firing arm around the outside of the leg and pulling the weapon in against the leg for support. Due to the low level of the weapon in this position, the sniper is forced to invert his head and has an almost upside down sight picture and reduced aperture, similar to that of the laid back position.
- **SITTING SUPPORTED:** The sniper uses this when some other form of support is available to carry the weight of the weapon, such as low cover or masonry. Here the sniper can use this aid to provide extra stability for his shot. However, with a fully floating barrel the sniper must be very careful not to rest the barrel in any way, since this will indeed affect the fall of shot.

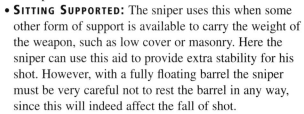

ABOVE: Here the sniper has modified the basic sitting position: his legs are crossed and ankles locked together, and he has pulled his elbows tighter into the inner leg area.

BELOW: A popular alternative to the basic sitting position, with the legs crossed but this time the arms are also crossed and resting on top of the knees in a cradle for the weapon.

ABOVE: Here the sniper actually looks through the scope upside down with the weapon locked into his upright leg for stability. It looks bizarre but is very stable up to 600m.

BELOW: A French Special Forces soldier attempts the laid back position. His weapon is the very effective PGM Commando, here with the suppressed barrel fitted.

THE KNEELING POSITION

This position is best used on level ground since any unevenness can lead to an unstable position and a loss of accuracy. It to can be modified in many different ways but the basic position follows the following parameters:

- **RIGHT FOOT:** The foot is placed in the most comfortable position possible with the sniper resting on his right knee and the foot rearwards. The right buttock then sits on the heel of the foot to avoid sitting too far back.
- **LEFT LEG:** The left leg is extended forward of the body with the toes pointing towards the intended target, foot flat on the ground. The non-firing elbow is rested on the left lower leg and the point of aim can be raised or lowered by movement of the left leg towards or away from the body.
- **RIGHT ELBOW:** The right elbow assumes a raised position to provide a natural cup to support the weapon butt.

KNEELING ALTERNATE

This position is very similar to the sitting alternate with the exception of the buttocks being off the ground. The head is still inverted and the left shin is still used as a support in conjunction with the non-firing arm that pulls it into the leg. This position requires practice and flexibility and if mastered will provide a very stable shooting platform over all ranges.

KNEELING SUPPORTED

This is as for the sitting supported and will use any available cover or object to aid the overall stability of the firing position.

ABOVE: The basic kneeling position. Unlike many of today's soldiers the sniper still makes good use of his sling to provide shooting stability.

BELOW: The kneeling supported position, the supporting hand resting against the tree with the weapon resting on the outstretched thumb.

ABOVE: The standing position is never going to be the sniper's first choice, but he must practise it for him to be fully effective. Here the sniper is using the cradle method to support the rifle, but before long this will become untenable and unstable because of the weight of the weapon.

ABOVE: With the standing supported position the sniper can at least distribute the weapon's as for the kneeling supported position.

BELOW: In the cradle position the sniper pulls in opposite directions with his arms to help brace them and give support to the rifle.

THE STANDING POSITION

The standing position is all too often ignored during training since it is inherently difficult and should be avoided where possible. But that does not mean it should be abandoned since it may well turn out to be the only option, and so it will pay to master the technique early. The standing position requires a greater level of upper body strength than other positions and the sniper's fitness training should not overlook this need. While this position can also be modified in various manners the basic stance is as follows:

- **FEET:** The feet should always be placed at a comfortable distance apart for the firer, and this is usually no more than shoulder width, with the feet angled approximately half right to the intended target.
- **RIFLE BUTT:** The weapon butt is held slightly higher in the shoulder in this position in order to bring the sight into line with the naturally higher eye line.
- **RIGHT ELBOW:** The elbow should be pulled tight into the body to aid the support of the rifle unless the sniper is engaging a moving target, where in which case it is sometimes better to keep the elbow higher and away from the body to avoid the tendency of pulling the barrel high right while tracking the target.
- **RIGHT HAND:** This hand will provide the rifle with most of its support and this is achieved with a firm grip on the weapon stock or pistol grip.

- **LEFT HAND:** This can either adopt the traditional position on the fore-stock or it can be clenched up and the arm bent at the elbow so as to rest the weapon along the top of the arm and hand. The elbow can be rested on the hip or webbing in order to distribute the rifle weight and help to maintain the position longer.

STANDING SUPPORTED

This, as with all other supported positions, will rely upon other aids that may be available to help provide the firer with a more stable position.

TRIGGER CONTROL

The effort of getting into a good, stable firing position can be lost in an instant if the sniper does not release the trigger at the correct time and in the correct manner. It is therefore essential that the sniper student is taught the fundamental skills of trigger control. The ability to release the shot without disturbing the aim is the basis of marksmanship and if the sniper cannot achieve this he will introduce inconsistency into his shooting and hence a loss of accuracy.

The action should be a smooth, continuous movement and not a sharp jerk. Jerking or snatching at the trigger is the most common fault in firers. Snatching is when the trigger is pulled too sharply and results in a disturbance of the position and the shot landing low right of the intended point of impact. The best leverage for trigger operation is to pull from low down on the trigger and to use the middle of the finger as opposed to the tip, but as long as the sniper is comfortable and consistently hits the target any operation is acceptable.

Various factors will affect the trigger operation and for the sniper to be effective it is essential that he is aware of these, this will instil a sense of self-diagnosis for all his shots. The most common is that of flinching. This is when the sniper anticipates the shot and shies away from it, causing the position to break. The most effective way of overcoming this is to load a mix of live and drill rounds when the sniper is on the range without him seeing the make-up of the magazine. Then his reactions are monitored when firing

to see if he is flinching when he gets to a drill round and pulls away expecting to hear the weapon report. With this identified he can be coached through his problem using the same method. However this type of drill must be monitored very carefully, with one instructor to each student to ensure range safety.

Another way to train for smooth trigger action is to place a coin on top of the barrel and get the sniper to operate the trigger. If the action is smooth the coin will stay in place; if not it will fall away from the barrel. The sniper will be taught that there are two types of trigger control and that once he has overcome any hang-ups such as flinching, he will always use one or the other.

These two types are "interrupted" and "uninterrupted":

- **INTERRUPTED:** This is when the pressure on the trigger has been started and there is a pause, when the pressure is maintained, before continuing the pressure take up until the moment of shot release. This is used with moving targets or when sight of the target is temporarily lost.
- **UNINTERRUPTED:** This is as the name suggests a continuous pressure on the trigger until the moment of shot release.

BREATHING

As with trigger operation, it is essential for the sniper to get his breathing correct prior to firing. The most natural time is that of the "natural respiratory pause". This is the point when the sniper has exhaled two-thirds of his lung capacity and has reached the natural pause in the breathing cycle, and is at his most relaxed. This period lasts for only a few seconds but can be extended to up to about eight seconds before

BELOW: In the urban situation the sniper has many solid objects with which to assist in supporting the weapon, but he must be careful to avoid resting the barrel on walls or fences which may affect the fall of shot. Here he uses his thumb.

ABOVE: A Gurkha sniper shooting a Parker-Hale sniper rifle. He uses the weapon's bipod to adjust to the required height he needs to engage his target, but he has to be aware of the increase in profile he presents the higher he goes.

the lack of oxygen will degrade the eyesight and induce discomfort and tension into the sniper, affecting the stability of his position.

This natural pause is the obvious point at which to release the shot and should also be used to perfect the aim, prior to taking two deep breaths to test and adjust the position before the moment of shot release. When breathing, the correct point of aim will lead to the cross hairs moving up and down over the target, with the point of aim being achieved at the natural pause. These techniques can only be mastered with constant practice with both live rounds and just as importantly with dry training drills.

GROUPING

It is essential that potential snipers can effectively shoot a tight group when zeroing their personnel weapons. If they cannot, then the likelihood of them being able to engage targets at distance is highly questionable. The definition of a group can best be explained as follows:

- A series of shots, not less than three, fired from the same point and at the same point of aim, will almost certainly never pass through the same hole and will more often produce a pattern of holes on the target, forming a group.

The reason that a poor grouper will be unlikely to hit targets at longer ranges is, according to the "theory of a group" that:

- The size of the group will increase in direct proportion to the range.

With this in mind, if the firer is able to achieve a group size of 4 inches (100mm) at 110 yards (100m) then at 660

ABOVE: A selection of targets used by the British Army in its sniper training programme, varying from the full image advancing soldier, through the half size semi-concealed advancing soldier, to the historically named (if not politically correct) "Huns head" target, and side-on runner.

yards (600m) he will be expected to group at 2 feet (600mm) and is unlikely to hit a man-sized target. He is then just not up to being trained as a sniper no matter how keen he may be.

FACTORS AFFECTING APPLICATION OF FIRE

It is important for the sniper to be aware of the factors that can affect his application of fire and this can be easily remembered be using the pneumonic **FLAPWIW**. This is a simple word that will prompt the sniper with sub headings of the factors he needs to monitor. The following are the main factors to remember:

F. FIRING POSITION: The mean point of impact (MPI) will vary slightly when firing from a different position from that in which the weapon was zeroed. This is caused by a combination of change in weapon harmonics, stability of position and different pressures being placed upon the rifle. Good, well built-up positions will reduce this effect.

L. LIGHT: The light levels will affect how he sees the target and the sniper must remember how various light conditions will affect his view of the target and aim accordingly.

A. ATTACHMENTS: Any attachment to the weapon will have an effect upon the weapon's harmonics and for any intended attachment the sniper should practice-fire the weapon and record the results, so as to provide him with settings for when he actually uses that attachment. Attachments can be night sights, lasers, foliage or hessian and all should be carefully checked before deploying on operations.

P. POSITIONAL SUPPORT: The sniper must be aware that

no matter what he uses to support the rifle, such as resting the weapon on his arm, the ground, a tripod, etc., it will have an effect on his MPI. Again he must train and record for this error. The sniper must never under any circumstances rest the barrel, since this will have a serious effect on his MPI.

W. WIND: There are various methods of reading and adjusting for wind and, whichever method is taught or preferred, the sniper must allow for the effects of wind on his shot.

I. INEFFICIENT ZERO: To cut corners or kid oneself at the zeroing stage of one's shooting is merely to guarantee a problem further down the line. If that happens to be on operations then it could be fatal.

W. WET OR OILY AMMUNITION: Wet or oily ammunition will cause an increase in chamber pressure that at worst will cause an explosion or can result in a bulge in the barrel leading to a loss of accuracy in the weapon. The very least it will do is increase muzzle velocity and thereby raise the MPI on the target.

OTHER AFFECTIHG FACTORS

TEMPERATURE

Under cold climate conditions the muzzle velocity will be decreased, causing a lowering of the initial MPI. However, each subsequent round will heat up the chamber and increase the muzzle velocity, and raise the MPI. The sniper must monitor for a climbing shot and adjust accordingly. Hot conditions will have the opposite effect whereby the heat will cause the charge to burn much quicker, increasing the pressure and velocity, leading to the rounds impacting higher on the target.

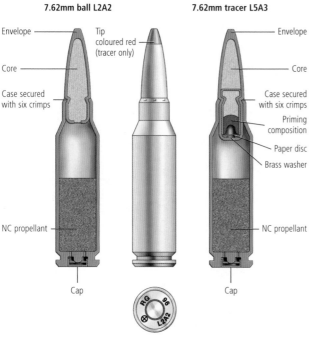

ABOVE: Various types of ammunition are supplied to snipers throughout the world. These are the different types available to the British sniper. The basic round is the 143-grain 7.62mm (308) which many feel is far too light to provide the long-range consistency required by the sniper. The round comes in armour-piecing and tracer form, although the sniper will never use the latter type of ammunition for obvious reasons. Also in the inventory is the 8.59mm (338 super Magnum) round which as well as having all the characteristics of the 7.62mm, is also available in armour-piecing incendiary (API) form, which is very useful to the sniper when engaging lightly armoured vehicles.

HUMIDITY

The amount of moisture in the air will increase the drag on the bullet as it passes through it. The more moisture, the greater the resistance, causing the round to impact low on the target.

RAIN

Heavy rain is always going to be a problem for the sniper. We already know the dramas caused by wet ammunition or weapon parts and so every effort should be made to keep the weapon and ammunition dry. If this is unavoidable then it is better to allow the weapon to get totally wet and compensate by lowering the elevation setting. A cover or rain shield can be made and applied to the front and rear of the scope to reduce the levels of water getting to the lens, and a cloth should always be carried by the sniper to assist in the removal of any rain that makes it to them.

MIRAGE

This is the effect of warm air rising off of the earth's surface in the form of currents, and is most visible on warm days. The mirage will indicate any air movement on days with light or no wind and can be seen as ripples or waves rising from the ground. The use of this effect to judge for deflection in such conditions takes much practice. For the experienced, mirage can provide an indication of the strength of the air's movement as well as its direction. With little or no wind the condition is known as boiling mirage; with any sideways movement it is called drift. The sniper has to remember that his shot will almost definitely fly over the mirage effect and so the mirage is of only limited use to him and it should only be used to confirm some other more reliable method. But at longer ranges the mirage can at least give the sniper an indication of some form of wind move-ment – whether it is straight up or moving sideways, say – at the target end.

CLOTHING

The sniper must be aware of how his clothing can affect his shooting ability and plan accordingly. The sniper MUST train from the very start of his shooting package in all of his operational ghillie outfit, inclusive of suit, gloves, headgear and webbing. Not to do this will produce a completely different set of results in his log book and hence will not be correct when applied on operations where the factors will have changed. This would seem to be an obvious point but many training teams overlook this and this leads to inconsistent shooting. The sniper must get used to his suit and modify it if necessary. He should produce a log book that gives the results and settings to be applied when he is wearing operational gear as opposed to results obtained while in comfortable uniform.

THE POOR-SHOOTING CHECK LIST

At some stage in his career the sniper will either have a bad day himself or will be training someone who could not hit a barn door with a Land Rover for no apparent reason. When this happens the first reference to call upon should be the poor-shooting check list:

- Sights are set correctly for elevation and deflection.
- The sight attachment screws are secure.
- The correct sight is fitted to the rifle.
- The sight drums are secure.
- The stock adjustments are secure.
- The bipod is not angled towards the target.
- The weapon is clean.

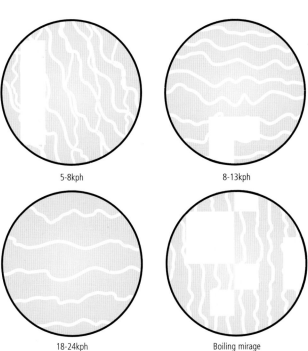

5-8kph   8-13kph

18-24kph   Boiling mirage

ABOVE: The sniper is trained to use the natural effect of mirage to judge the wind direction and speed when shooting. When mastered after much practice this becomes a very reliable method. The diagram above illustrates the main wind speeds indicated by the mirage's direction when viewed through the sniper's telescopic sight.

ABOVE: With the wrong eye relief in relation to the telescopic sight the fall of shot will be adversely affected. This is known as a "floating aperture".

Correct eye relief = correct aim   Incorrect eye relief = floating aperture

ABOVE: What the sniper sees through his optics. When the sniper has the correct eye relief he will have a clear, even image of his target. However, should he adopt the incorrect eye relief he will see a dark image around or to the side of his target. This should be a warning to him that he needs to correct his position before firing.

If all of the above present no problems then the sniper/instructor should get an experienced firer to shoot the weapon to check if it is the weapon or the firer that is at fault, or have an armourer carry out an inspection of the rifle.

OPERATIONAL SNAP SHOOTING

In operations, the sniper will invariably be patrolling in close proximity to the enemy and may on occasion need to engage them at short notice. To do this the sniper must make the most of the flatter trajectory of the closer ranges and set his sights on 330 yards (300m). The reason for this is that at this setting the sniper can aim at the centre of a man-sized target at any range between 110 and 440 yards (100 and 400m), and, due to the flatter trajectory, he can expect to hit the target.

THE MISS DRILL

If the sniper finds that he is missing the target he must locate his fall of shot in order to adjust on to the target. To do this the sniper and his observer can use one of the following methods:

• **STRIKE/SPLASH:** This is the ground kicked up by the bullet's impact, indicating the fall of shot.
• **SWIRL:** This is the air that is displaced by the bullet as it travels towards the target and is seen as a swirling vortex that indicates the bullet's path.
• **GLINT:** Under certain conditions it is possible to see a glint of light reflected off the bullet as it travels through the air, and this, although brief, will indicate the likely fall of shot.

BELOW: A British sniper pair training on the range. The firer is using the very stable and unorthodox inverted head position. Note how "un-human" he looks from a camouflage point of view, as he would appear to have no head!

• **TRACER:** Tracer rounds can be used as a last resort, but this is not favoured by snipers and is not a recommended method since the tracer round damages the weapon bore and may lead to loss of accuracy.

WIND ALLOWANCE

The sniper must understand the wind's effects and also be able to make allowances for its influence in order to hit his intended target, especially over the greater distances that he will shoot. Learning all about the wind's effects and how to allow for it will take the sniper many hours of practice, and the keeping of an accurate log book with details of different types of wind effect will assist in building up a solid database for future shoots.

The wind will affect the sniper in two ways when shooting – first, by affecting the firer's ability to hold the weapon stable prior to shot release, and second by affecting the bullet as it passes through the air. The effects upon the sniper's ability to hold the weapon can be offset with the adoption of a suitably stable fire position, and the sniper must select the position that will allow this and still fit the operational scenario. But the ability to judge for effect on the bullet will take more time to master.

The wind effect at the target end is often misleading. By the time the bullet has reached that point, it has already been affected, and so the sniper needs to judge the wind within the first half of the bullet's journey in order to compensate. There are four main factors that the sniper will have to allow for when calculating the wind effect on his shot and they are:

• Wind strength (velocity).
• Wind direction.
• Range to the target.
• The bullet (size, weight and velocity).

WIND STRENGTH

The wind's strength has to be determined so that the sniper can calculate its effect on his shot. There are generally five recognised wind strengths that are used in these equations:

• Gentle – 5mph (8kph), wind barely felt but detectable.
• Moderate – 10mph (16kph), wind felt lightly on the face, leaves and twigs moving.
• Fresh – 15mph (24kph), wind moves dust, paper and small branches on trees in constant motion.
• Strong – 20mph (32kph), wind moves the majority of the tree.
• Very Strong – 25+mph (40+kph), wind moves large trees, telephone wires hum in the wind, large waves form at sea.

The sniper must learn to determine the wind type and there are several aids available to him to assist in this task. The first method is that of simple observation of the battle-field around him and the recognition of how the wind is affecting different items. The most obvious item is that of the foliage at varying points along the intended path of the bullet, since this will give an indication of the wind's strength and direction between the sniper and his intended target. Indeed, the sniper can utilise any objects along the path that are being influenced by the wind to give an indication as to the likely effect at any given point.

Another method is to drop some grass from the firing point and observe the angle at which it falls to the ground. This however will only indicate the wind at the firing point and not at any point along the bullet's flight-path, and so is

ABOVE: British and French snipers share a range in France. The Briton (closest to camera) is using the AI 338 super magnum rifle while the French sniper is using the FRF2.

of limited value. Furthermore there appears to be no tactical sense in standing to drop grass from a concealed firing position, and to drop grass from the prone position will yield little result!

The other, often quoted, method is that of noting the angle of the range flag. This is no doubt very useful on the range or to all the "paper-shooters" out there whose "sniper" experience is limited to the number of competitions they have attended this year, but the author has yet to find an enemy who is thoughtful enough to put up range indication flags for the sniper's use. So it needs to be remembered that this method can be a useful *training* vehicle but will be of no use on operations.

WIND VALUES

The wind direction will also have an effect on the bullet in flight and so is just as important as the strength. To value this the easiest method to use is the "clock method". This places an imaginary clock over the sniper's view and is broken down into sections, with each section having a different wind value dependent upon its effect on the bullet's flight-path. The direction that will have the most effect on the bullet is that of a wind blowing left to right or right to left across the bullet's path, and therefore will be valued the highest or "full value". This will be 3 to 9 or 9 to 3 on the clock face. For winds blowing at oblique angles such as from 1 to 7 or from 11 to 5 a value of half the right to left

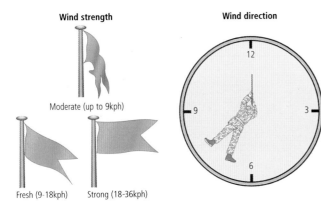

Wind strength

Moderate (up to 9kph)

Fresh (9-18kph)   Strong (18-36kph)

Wind direction

12

9   3

6

ABOVE: The sniper has to make allowances for wind strength and direction at his own position all the way to the target. Tell-tale signs will be the obvious ones of the strength of the wind on the face, disturbance of dust and debris, and movement of trees

and other vertical objects, and the effect on water at sea or on lakes. Before making adjustments for wind strength and direction, which takes much practice, factors also to be borne in mind are range to the target and bullet size, weight and velocity.

wind is given or "half value". For winds that blow into the sniper's face or over him and in the same direction as the intended shot a zero value is given as these will have little if any effect on the bullet's path.

Most armies issue their snipers with a wind calculation table to assist in wind calculations. These are generally committed to memory by the sniper. They follow a simple formula with the range, wind direction and strength all laid out in a simple graph format that enables the sniper to quickly equate the solution he needs. For oblique winds he simply halves the total he reached on his calculation for a "full value" wind.

MOVING TARGETS

The ideal target, when shooting over any sort of distance, is a static one and ideally in a "no wind" condition, but that is often not the case. More frequently the sniper is engaging a moving target that he loses sight of every couple of seconds, and so the sniper must be competent with both the static and moving target in order for him to be effective.

As with normal shooting practices, there are two main methods of engaging moving targets – the "ambush" method and the "tracking" method.

AMBUSH METHOD

With this method the sniper selects a point ahead of the target's direction of travel and releases the shot when the lead is reached for that particular target.

TRACKING METHOD

This method involves the sniper aligning with the required lead for the target, maintaining it and releasing the shot when ready, ensuring that he follows through the shot, otherwise the shot will strike to the rear of the target and miss.

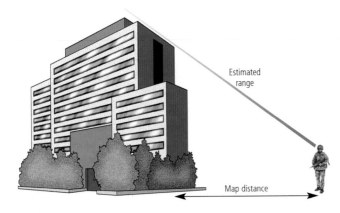

Estimated range

Map distance

ABOVE Estimating target distance from height. The formula is estimated range x cosine of slope = map distance. Here, with a

slope of 30deg, the calculation is: range 475yd (434m) x slope cosine (.87) = map distance of 413yd (377m).

BELOW: A British and German sniper work as a pair during a sniper instructor course in the UK. Note how the firer is using

the tree to support the weight of the rifle while avoiding resting the barrel, which could adversely affect his shot.

COMMON ERRORS

Engaging moving targets is a difficult skill and, as with many areas of sniping, it requires dedicated practice. There are some common mistakes that, once identified, can be overcome. These errors are as follows:

- A tendency to jerk or snatch the trigger at the moment of shot release. This is caused by the sniper anticipating the shot and trying to "force" the shot. It is most common in the "ambush" technique.
- Failure to add adjustments for deflection to allow for wind influence. Many snipers overlook this area when pre-occupied with the moving target.
- The sniper focusing on the target and not the sight reticule, and hence not paying attention to his lead point within the sight's reticule pattern.

All of these points can be easily remedied and just require the sniper to think a bit harder about the basics of engaging distance targets and to not be seduced by the moving target.

TARGET LEADS

The leads (aiming ahead of the target) taken for moving targets will vary from firer to firer. People have different levels of reaction and trigger pull upon the location of their target. However, there is a general starting system that is applied by many of the world's snipers. This system is very similar to that used in the calculation of the wind's effects and follows the principle of identifying start values for walking targets, with these values being doubled for a running target and halved for an oblique target.

This method allows for a 5 MOA (minutes of angle) lead for a walking man at ranges of 400, 500 and 600 yards (366, 457 and 549m) and can be applied by aiming ahead of the target or by applying the calculation to the sight and maintaining point of aim/point of impact. The settings for a moving target must be applied only after allowance has been made for the effects of the wind. To allow for a moving target, the sniper may have to remove some of the setting

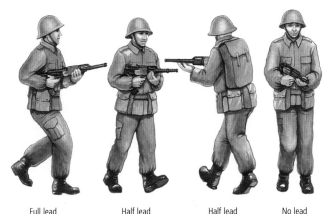

Full lead   Half lead   Half lead   No lead

ABOVE: When shooting at moving targets the sniper must take into account the distance and the wind speed and direction, as well as the angle and speed at which the target is moving. To ensure a first round hit the sniper will allow the target a degree of lead, so that the target and the round reach the same point at the same time. Success in this will be determined by the above calculations combined with the factors of the weapon and ammunition.

applied for wind affects, for example, a man moving at walking speed (5 MOA) travelling right to left across the sniper's view would cancel out an adjustment of 5 MOA added for a left to right wind. This method allows the sniper to aim at the centre of the target and maintain point of aim/point of impact.

AIMING OFF

These adjustments are again calculated for a walking target and need to be doubled for fast targets and halved for oblique targets accordingly. Using the 5-MOA method, the sniper will take the first figure of the range to the target and multiply by 5 to give the lead required. For example, 5 x 600 yards = 30 inch lead (5 x 549m = 76cm lead). As with the previous method, adjustments for wind are applied first, and then adjustments are applied for movers with the aim point at the required position ahead of the target.

SHOOTING AIDS

The sniper should be taught to shoot from many and varied positions so as to increase the chances of him being able to locate a suitable fire position no matter what the environmental surroundings. Some armies, however, seem pre-occupied with the prone position, firing off a rucksack. While this is indeed a very stable position, it is not often practical due to vegetation or man-made obstacles such as walls or buildings. There is, therefore, a need to explore and to practise firing from as many positions as possible, and under all conditions, with the results being accurately recorded in the sniper's log book for future reference.

With positions away from the prone or supported, the sniper will find it increasingly difficult to maintain a stable shooting position for his weapon. Any assistance in this area should be considered. An abundance of weapon supports are now available to the civilian hunter or shooter and could, under certain circumstances, be of use to the sniper. These weapon supports vary from collapsible bipods and tripods to very substantial and superbly stable shooting platforms, such as those made by the American firm Center Mass, Inc. This company offers a wide range of very stable weapon rests that can greatly enhance the snipers shooting over distance and should definitely be looked at, as an option should the mission allow. However, it is highly improbable that the military sniper would ever find a way to take such luxury items with him, given their size and weight. For the police marksman, who does not have the problems of the military sniper, the addition of one of these rests to his deployment vehicle is a must, since the stability provided for drawn-out negotiated scenarios, where a sudden but highly accurate shot is required, cannot be underestimated. For military anti-terrorist units who find themselves in long duration intelligence-gathering missions but are also expected to shoot with little warning, should the scenario dictate, these weapon rests are a wise purchase.

The military sniper will seldom get the chance to use such precision-crafted shooting aids. His world is a much harsher one and these items are just too big for sniper deployment. For him the word "improvise" comes once more to the fore and again the sniper must create, from what is around him, the luxuries the police marksman takes for granted.

The answer that both the US and British Forces have come up with is two-fold. Some choose to add a normal

ABOVE AND RIGHT: For the law enforcement and anti-terrorist marksman who does not have to worry about stalking with all his kit, a vice-like weapon mount is a favourable. One of the best from Center Mass, Inc., whose Tactical Sharpshooter Rifle Rest allows the firer to set up his weapon to take just about any angle shot.

camera tripod to their kit, with its light weight and height adjusting legs, and simply add a weapon rest to the camera platform made out of the multi-use sticky tape (known as "black and nasty" in the UK military) and sponge. This will provide a good working platform from which to shoot, but is somewhat impractical in so much as it is awkward and cumbersome to carry, particularly so during stalking under operational conditions. For urban operations, however, it may be worth the extra burden to provide the sniper with a ready-made rest that can be sighted deep within a room.

The other option most often used is that of cutting three suitably sturdy branches from around the area of operations and binding them together with para cord approximately one-third down from the top of the branches. These can then be spread out to form a tripod on which to rest the rifle in order to provide a quick and sturdy rest from which to take the shot. The length of the branches will depend on the position the sniper intends to adopt, which in turn will be dictated by the available cover around his final fire position

BELOW: For the military sniper the most practical option is to cut three lengths of timber and tie them together to form a rest. Here, British snipers use their improvised rests to stabilise their binoculars on a range estimation lesson.

(FFP). When using this method the sniper must ensure that he cuts the branches away from the FFP and if possible from a concealed position so as to not leave any indication or ground sign for the enemy to locate, otherwise this may indicate the sniper's method of operation and endanger him or his colleagues at a later date.

SUPPRESSED CAPABILITY

The additional ability to fire rounds with reduced noise levels is one that all snipers should have. Indeed, most of the world's current sniper rifles are available in suppressed versions. Such shooting is commonly linked to the world of special forces and assassins but, if looked at it in a realistic and tactical way, it becomes obvious why the sniper should have a suppressed capability with him on all deployments. The sniper often passes within feet of the enemy or has to move past an enemy to reach his target, and so the ability to limit the number of people who hear his shot will limit the number of people who come looking for him, and hence greatly increase his life expectancy. To add this capability to the sniper's armoury would not cost very much at all when you consider the cost of the average armoured vehicle. For internal security or terrorist-related operations, where the world's media are hunting a military mistake, a suppressed capability is invaluable. The suppressed sniper rifle is a strange beast and one that takes a lot of practice to master, but once mastered it is just as devastating in effect as its full-

ABOVE: The Tactical Suppressed AI sniper rifle offers the sniper the advantage of firing full power or sub-sonic ammunition, and greatly increases his survival rate.

bore brother, maybe more so. To see someone drop and yet hear nothing can be a psychological shock. If this capability is to be added to the sniper's list of options then he must be allowed the time and ammunition to practise as much as he does with normal full-power bullets. Such practice must also be added to his log book to facilitate future "cold shots" from his records.

DESTRUCTION DRILLS

All snipers must be taught how to destroy their weapons in the event of impending capture or having to abandon the rifle. This is to remove the ability of the enemy to use those weapons against the sniper's own forces. The following are effective methods of rendering a rifle useless:

- Block the barrel with earth, metal or anything that will do the job, push the muzzle into the ground and, using string to operate the trigger, fire the weapon.
- Strip the weapon and hide or bury parts over a wide area.
- Strip the weapon and keep essential parts separated from the abandoned rifle.
- Take any steps necessary to bend the barrel, smash the telescopic sights and destroy the weapon's accuracy.

CURRENT OPERATIONAL SNIPER WEAPONS

We will now look at the current crop of issued military sniper rifles. It would be impossible to cover all available weapons currently found around the world, especially as the ex-Warsaw Pact countries are now producing numerous variations on their old models to bolster their flagging economies. So we will focus on the main types in general service.

ACCURACY INTERNATIONAL (UK)

L96A1
CALIBRE: 7.62 x 51MM NATO
MUZZLE VELOCITY: 2756FT/SEC (840M/SEC) (COVERT VERSION 1,033FT/SEC (315M/SEC)
WEIGHT: 14.33LB (6.5KG)
BARREL: 25.78IN (655MM), 4 GROOVES, RH TWIST, ONE TURN IN 12IN (305MM)
MAGAZINE: 10 ROUND

SUPER MAGNUM
CALIBRE: .338
MUZZLE VELOCITY: 3,000FT/SEC (914 M/SEC)
WEIGHT: 15LB (6.8KG)
BARREL: 27IN (686MM)
MAGAZINE: 4 ROUND

In the 1980s the British Army approached industry to produce a replacement for the long serving L42 Lee Enfield rifle. One of the companies approached was Accuracy International, which had the British Olympic Gold shooting medallist Malcolm Cooper at the helm. The company came up with a design that left traditions far behind and drew more than one criticism for basing the design on a central frame that had a removable high impact plastic stock attached, but which could still function without it. The design also allowed for the quick and easy replacement of barrel and locking ring although the barrels have been proved to hold their accuracy for over 5000 rounds without losing operational effectiveness. The weapon was accepted into British service in 1986 and issued to the Army infantry, Royal Marines and special forces and has seen active service in all theatres involving the UK since that date. The initial weapon was designated the L96A1 in British service and this rifle was sold to over twenty countries worldwide in its original form.

In the late 1980s the Swedish military put out a tender for a new sniper weapon and AI submitted their "updated" L96A1 in the shape of the AW, or Arctic Warfare, which, after stringent tests, was accepted into Swedish service and very quickly accepted thereafter into Belgian service also. The AW has a special ice-resistant bolt that allows operation in temperatures down to –40 degrees C and the barrel is guaranteed to maintain a hit in a 3/4-inch (20mm) target at 110 yards (100m) using sniper ammunition. With this success, the L96A1 was removed from production and the AW, with modifications coming from experience gained in operational deployments of the L96A1, became the standard production rifle of AI.

AI also produced different variations of the basic AW with both fully and tactically suppressed versions available and a special Covert version that folded to fit into a large suitcase with all its accessories for special purpose force use and police deployments. The company continue to update their basic rifle and to meet customer needs and have recently added folding-stock versions and a very impressive .50 calibre AW50 based on the AW design to their

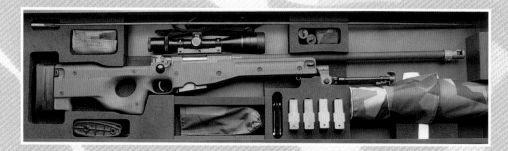

LEFT: AI AW rifle in transit case with associated ancillaries. Note the weapon valise in Swedish military camouflage.

BELOW: An AW with white furniture and a fluted barrel, among many modifications available with AI weapons.

ABOVE: The AI AW with tactical suppressor and folding stock. AI weapons have been market leaders for 15 years.

RIGHT: Latest AI sniper weapon is the monster, but comparatively light, bolt-action AW .50 calibre rifle.

selection. The larger-calibred .338 Super Magnum version has added an even harder-hitting option to the basic AW and has recently been accepted into British Army service and issued to the 16 Air Assault Brigade. The author has used AI's weapons now for many years and, having tested and fired other sniper rifles from many countries, believes that this is the best option available. With sales of the weapon to over thirty-five countries worldwide, it appears to be the opinion of many others as well.

M40A1/A2/A3 (USA: US MARINE CORPS)

M40A1
CALIBRE: 7.62 x 51MM
MUZZLE VELOCITY: 2,540FT/SEC (775M/SEC)
WEIGHT: 14.5LB (6.57KG)
BARREL: 24IN (610MM), 4 GROOVES, RH TWIST, ONE TURN IN 12IN (305MM)
MAGAZINE: 5 ROUND

The US Marine Corps, with its fine traditions in marksmanship, took the selection of the Springfield M1903 sniper rifle replacement very seriously and had clear ideas on what was needed. After a brief look at the US Army M21, a sniper version of the semi-automatic M14, the Marines opted for a version of the Remington 700 series rifle chambered for the NATO 7.62 x 51mm round.

The Marine armourers made several modifications to the basic design, covering colour and sight selection, where the choice was for the x10 powered Unertl scope, and kept the design to the basic hunting rifle format, avoiding the likes of synthetic stocks or bipods as was the trend in other countries.

All in all, the Marines were issued a very strong, accurate and robust sniper weapon that went on to serve with distinction all over the world in the hands of the very professional Marine snipers. This weapon was backed up by what the author feels must be the most comprehensive workshop maintenance schedule anywhere in the world with all the Corps' rifles being constantly serviced on a scale

that would put a vehicle mechanic to shame – which, when considering that a man's life is at stake, can be no bad thing.

Over the years since its acceptance the M40A1 has been modified twice, bringing it up to the current M40A3 version. This is still the basic rifle that has served the Marine sniper so well but it now has a synthetic stock that allows an individual to adjust the weapon to fit him, and the addition of a detachable bipod to assist in rifle stability when shooting.

Certain "older" members of the Marine Corps would have been grave reservations about these "new-fangled" modifications, and doubtless these objections will rage for many years to come, but the Marine sniper still has a very robust and accurate rifle that the author has been privileged to use on several occasions. If an AW was not available, this would be his weapon of choice to take to war.

ABOVE: The M40 series are the tried and tested weapons of the US Marine Corps.

BELOW: The M40A1 fitted with the very effective SIMRAD night sight.

IRON BRIGADE ARMORIES CHANDLER SNIPER RIFLE (USA)

CHANDLER SNIPER RIFLE
CALIBRE: 7.62 x 51MM NATO
WEIGHT: 15LB (6.8KG)
BARREL: 26IN (660MM), 6 GROOVES, RH TWIST, ONE TURN IN 12IN (305MM)
MAGAZINE: 5 ROUND

The Iron Brigade company is run by retired US Marine Corps Colonel Norman Chandler, whom the author is lucky enough to know as a friend. One of Chandler's commands was that of the Marine Weapon Training Battalion at Stone Bay, Camp Lejeune, so he was party to many discussions on the wants and wishes of Marine Corps shooters. Accordingly he has produced what he believes to be a very accurate sniper rifle based around the tried and tested M40A1.

The rifle uses the Remington M700 receiver, a 26in (660mm) Hart barrel, a McMillan stock and a selection of Leupold telescopic sights. The author has not fired the weapon, but has been assured by a very close friend and Master Sniper of the US Marine Corps, Msgt Neil Morris, that this rifle is indeed a very accurate and well-balanced weapon and one that could hold its own against any rifle.

RIGHT: The author has tested the Chandler sniper rifle, which is based around the US Marine M40A1, and considers that it has been manufactured to very high standard.

PARKER-HALE M85 (USA)

PARKER-HALE M85
CALIBRE: 7.62 x 51MM NATO.
MUZZLE VELOCITY: 2,890FT/SEC (880M/SEC)
WEIGHT: 12.57LB (5.7KG)
BARREL: 27.5IN (700MM) 4 GROOVES, RH TURN, ONE TURN IN 12IN (305MM)
MAGAZINE: 10 ROUND

This UK-based weapon manufacturer was bought out by the US firm, Navy Arms, in 1990. While the M85 is a totally US-made rifle, its design dates from the British Army requirement for a new

ABOVE: The author trialing the Parker-Hale M85 sniper rifle while in the Falklands running sniper training for the Gurkhas. It proved to be a very accurate weapon.

sniper weapon that led to the adoption of the AI L96A1. The rifle was not chosen for the UK forces but it did achieve limited success and the author recently came across one in the Falkland Island Defence Force. The weapon was based on the M82 design that was accepted by the forces of Australia, New Zealand and Canada (all of whom have replaced it with AI weapons) and came in a variety of stock colours to suit the buyer. The rifle could be fitted with a bipod and was able to take a suppressor if needed, and is a very accurate sniper rifle.

STEYR SSG (AUSTRIA)

STEYR SSG

CALIBRE: 7.62 x 51MM NATO
MUZZLE VELOCITY: 2,820FT/SEC (860M/SEC)
WEIGHT: 8.6LB (3.9KG)
BARREL: 25.6IN (650MM), 4 GROOVES, RH TWIST
MAGAZINE: 5 ROUND

The SSG is another traditionally designed sniper weapon with 1960s vintage, but is still a very effective sniper rifle. The author also discovered one of these rifles in the Falklands recently and had the chance to fire it over various ranges, finding it to be a very reliable and accurate little weapon. The rifle has no frills and is very basic in design, but its light weight and small size made it a pleasure to stalk with, and its accuracy was not to be underestimated. The basic design was accepted into the Austrian military in the 1960s and several other versions were made, including both suppressed and police models. The weapon is to be found all over the world today, confirming its sound design and reliability.

BELOW: The Steyr SSG (nearest to camera) next to the Parker-Hale M85. This small and light rifle is a very accurate and deceptively sturdy sniper weapon.

HECKLER & KOCH MSG-90 (UK)

HK MSG-90

CALIBRE: 7.62 x 51MM NATO
MUZZLE VELOCITY: 2,788FT/SEC (850M/SEC)
WEIGHT: 14LB (6.4KG)
BARREL: 23.6IN (600MM) 4 GROOVES, RH TWIST
MAGAZINE: 5 OR 20 ROUND

This well-known German company was bought out by the British Royal Ordnance firm in the 1990s and while the German-based factories still function the production is split between the UK and Germany, with both sides producing HK and RO weaponry. The HK MSG-90 was produced as a military sniper rifle from the start as opposed to the company's PSG-1 weapon that is an out-and-out police rifle, unsuited to military applications, although very effective. The MSG takes the basic G3 format but is built to much more stringent standards and has the standard NATO sight mount that allows the fitting of most optical sights to suit the end user. The weapon is very robust and uses a semi-automatic system, unlike most of the world's sniper weapons. In certain countries it is regarded as an observer's weapon to back up a more conventional bolt-action sniper weapon, rather than as the first choice sniper rifle. This is not to say that is not accurate enough, as it most def-initely is, but just that most doctrines teach "fire one round and then move position to avoid detection", and the speedy second shot that the MSG offers is not often needed. The author was able to use this weapon while working alongside the US Marine snipers who were considering the weapon's suitability as a dedicated marksman rifle for issue to sharpshooters as opposed to snipers, who were more than happy with their M40s.

RIGHT: The author firing the HK MSG-90. He found it very accurate and strong, but too heavy and cumbersome to be a military sniper weapon deployed for all out operations.

DRAGUNOV SVD (RUSSIA)

DRAGUNOV SVD
CALIBRE: 7.62 x 54R
MUZZLE VELOCITY: 2,723FT/SEC (830M/SEC)
WEIGHT: 9.5LB (4.3KG)
BARREL: 24.5IN (622MM) 4 GROOVES, RH TWIST, ONE TURN IN 10IN
(254MM)
MAGAZINE: 10 ROUND

The rumours of a new sniper weapon being issued to Soviet troops and allies in the 1960s caused a lot of concern in the West, and the "acquiring" of one became a top priority. This happened only in the early stages of the Vietnam War when a Russian sniper, operating with a Vietnamese partner, was killed by US troops and he was found to be using the then-new Dragunov SVD rifle. The Dragunov was found to be of semi-automatic format and both accurate and reliable when tested, being built around the basic Kalashnikov mechanism and the old 7.62 x 54 rimmed round of 185 grain. It was a very advanced design for its time and was indeed a very sturdy sniper weapon, with good accuracy over long range and the robustness of construction needed for prolonged sniper work. The rifle could take any Soviet sighting system, but was usually to be found with the PSO-1 4 x 24 magnification sight fitted, which had some very useful features that western sights did not. These included a simple range finding stadia within the sniper's view that assisted in judging the distance to the intended target, and an illuminated sight reticule for low light conditions. While the weapon may have looked like it was made from an old trashcan, it was very strong and durable.

The author was able to fire this weapon on several occasions, one kindly donated by the IRA being the first, and found it to be an accurate and comfortable rifle to use with a good sense of balance to it. The rifle has been produced under license in several countries including former Warsaw Pact members and China and has been produced in modified versions, and acted as the start point for many other rifles. But the basic original is still in use and still very effective today. While several "special purpose" sniper weapons have emerged within the Russian military, the SVD is still the issued rifle to the main forces.

ABOVE: The author found the Dragunov to be a very reliable rifle that could hold its own in the accuracy stakes. It is a well balanced rifle that is very comfortable to use.

BELOW: The Dragunov less its telescopic sight in an American armoury! It would normally be fitted with a PSO-1 4 x 24 sighting system or any other former Soviet system.

ABOVE: The Dragunov rifle displayed with spare magazines, oil bottle and cleaning kit. The sling left a lot to be desired, but then you can't have everything!

VSS Silent Sniper Rifle (Russia)

VSS Silent Sniper Rifle
Calibre: 9 x 39mm
Muzzle velocity: approx. 1,080ft/sec (330m/sec)
Weight: 5.7lb (2.6kg)
Barrel: length not known, construction based on the double chamber system
Magazine: 10 or 20 round

Over the last few years, with the Russian arms manufacturers entering into the general market and the traditional secrecy associated with Russian weapons all but gone, there have been a multitude of Kalashnikov-based weapons offered for purchase. These have ranged from under-water assault rifles, firing steel darts at an alarming rate, to so-called silent sniper rifles. The VSS is billed as a silent sniper rifle but one look at it would suggest it is in the DeLisle sentry-removing weapon category as opposed to being a true long-range sniper rifle. It has an integral barrel/suppressor unit that it is claimed has greater range and penetrating power than other similar systems. The rifle is based around a 9 x 39mm Special Purpose round that gets its heritage from the M1943 case enlarged to take a 16.3g bullet that has a hardened core and tip which is claimed to have a high degree of armour penetration, including .08 inches at 550 yards (2mm at 500m). With the round being sub-sonic and the known fact that sub-sonic rounds take a very curved trajectory to their target, it is hard to see how this round or weapon can claim such accuracy and penetration over this distance with the optical sighting systems seen with it. The weapon has been photographed in the hands of Russian troops working along side US forces in Kosovo recently, and so it is reasonable to assume that the West now knows more about this rifle than it did before. The author would not put it in the same class as the Dragunov and would again suggest its role lies in the area of special forces and not that of the sniper.

FRF1/FRF2 (France)

FRF1/FRF2
Calibre: 7.62 x 51mm NATO
Muzzle velocity: 2,790ft/sec (850m/sec)
Weight: 11.5lb (5.2kg)
Barrel: 21.7in (552mm), 4 grooves, RH twist, one turn in 12in (305mm)
Magazine: 10 round

Above: The FRF2 sniper weapon with the issued MAS sidearm. It proved to be fairly accurate but is let down by its optics that are more in line with sharpshooting than sniping.

The French decided that they would base their requirement for a sniper rifle on the reliable MAS 36 action and so they built up the very successful FRF1 and introduced it into the French forces in the 1960s. The rifle had a wooden half-stock with adjustable butt length and a longer, more accurate barrel than the MAS 36. It was fitted with the Modèle 53bis telescopic sight that was heavily based on a German World War II design. It also came with an integral bipod that, while adjustable, was limited in its effectiveness.

The weapon was originally chambered for the French 7.5 x 54mm round but has since been changed to the NATO 7.62 x 51mm cartridge for standardisation with NATO deployments. Over the years operational experience has led to several modifications, and in 1984 the French introduced the FRF2 to replace the FRF1s as they became unserviceable. The new rifle was in essence the FRF1 but with a couple of changes: the stock was now synthetic, the bipod was slightly realigned, and the barrel was concealed in a black thermal sleeve to reduce heat effects on the barrel and the sight picture and to reduce the rifle's thermal signature, thus making it more difficult to locate. Recently the French have introduced a newer optical sight that is a vast improvement on the older version, and the author experienced them both while working alongside French armoured and airborne troops in recent years.

PGM Commando and Hecate (France)

PGM COMMANDO
CALIBRE: 7.62 x 51MM NATO
MUZZLE VELOCITY: 950FT/SEC (290M/SEC)
WEIGHT: 12LB (5.5KG)
BARREL: THREE VARIATIONS
MAGAZINE: 5 ROUND

PGM HECATE
CALIBRE: .50IN (12.7 x 99MM)
MUZZLE VELOCITY: 2,705FT/SEC (825M/SEC)
WEIGHT: 30.4LB (13.8KG)
BARREL: 27.5IN (700MM)
MAGAZINE: 7 ROUND

The author was also fortunate enough to handle and fire both the PGM Commando and the .50-calibre Hecate while recently deployed with French units. Both rifles are very accurate and user friendly. They have a skeleton frame, similar to the AI design, with modular attachments completing the weapon. The Commando version is chambered for the NATO 7.62 x 51mm round and features a quick change barrel system that allows the selection of an 18in (457mm), 23.6in (600mm) or suppressed barrel dependent upon the mission. This can all be done in the field with no more than a 5mm Allen key. The rifle, as with recent AW versions, is supplied with a folding stock to allow for airborne insertions or for the covert insertion where the rifle needs to be hidden from view. The Hecate is the "daddy" of the family and was recently beaten into second place by the AI 338 Super Magnum in a very close fought competition for the British Army Long Range Large Calibre requirement, proving it to be a very capable rifle. It follows the basic construction format of the other PGMs but has a fluted barrel to help reduce the overall weight. The rifle has a very effective muzzle break that greatly reduces the stress and strain on the firer associated with weapons of this calibre. It is supplied with an integral bipod and monopod to hold the rifle in position for longer periods. This again reduces the workload of the firer. The rifle can use any .50 Browning ammunition but to achieve the weapon's maximum accurate range of 1,650yd (1,500m) it is advisable to use hand-loaded ball rounds.

ABOVE: The PGM Commando was found to be an effective and versatile weapon system. The system has a folding stock and interchangeable barrels and was very accurate.

BELOW: The PGM also comes in a .50 version known as the Hecate and this weapon was narrowly beaten in a British shoot-off competition by the AI 338 Super Magnum.

BARRETT M82A1 "LIGHT FIFTY" (USA)

BARRETT LIGHT FIFTY
CALIBRE: .50IN (12.7 x 99MM)
MUZZLE VELOCITY: 2,788FT/SEC (850M/SEC)
WEIGHT: 28.44LB (12.9KG)
BARREL: 29IN (737MM)
MAGAZINE: 10 ROUND

This rifle was really the first large-calibre rifle to be touted around the sniper world and as such has become the benchmark for other systems. The rifle, while being capable of devastating anti-personnel roles, is primarily used for anti-materiel work, where radars, aircraft, armoured vehicles or missile systems are the targets and not their operators. With the need to engage these targets from extreme range, the sniper was the obvious man to take on the role, although with targets as big as aircraft most competent shooters could cope, and so the Barrett picked up its sniper rifle tag. The use of it by the IRA in Northern Ireland to shoot both

soldiers and police officers at very short range (never more than 275 yards (250m)) also gave the weapon a worldwide notoriety when the world's media slapped a "sniper" label on the terrorists taking the shots. They obviously were not and soon ran scared when professional snipers deployed to stop them. Thus, however, the legend of the Barrett "Lght Fifty" was born. The weapon proved to be effective enough in its main role and has been used by several countries, in both the anti-materiel and unexploded ordnance removal roles, with great success. The rifle is easy to use and comfortable to fire. It can be mounted on ground vehicles or helicopter mounts, thus providing a wide range of deployment options, and can be found in many of the world's armouries, including at least one British police force! The use of such large calibres is no new thing, as the use of the Boys' anti-tank rifle of World War II illustrates but there is definitely a trend towards reintroducing them and at present there are calibres varying from 12.7mm up to 20mm on the market. With such competition, it has to be of credit that the Barrett is still right up there with its rivals.

ABOVE: The author firing the .50 Barrett rifle on a field firing range. The weapon is big, strong and hard-hitting, primarily used for anti-materiel work rather than for other snipers.

BELOW: A US Marine Corps Barrett rifle painted in a scheme considered suitable for Marine deployment. It is used by Force Recon Marines and other special forces.

BARRETT LIGHT FIFTY

TACTICAL DEPLOYMENT

The sniper has for many years been the most feared man on the battlefield and looks to remain that way for the foreseeable future. This has mainly been as a result of two things – the common knowledge of the sniper's shooting skills, and the fear of never knowing where he is or what he can see. The sniper selects individual targets, unlike the less "personal" effects of artillery and machine gun fire; couple that to the fear of not knowing where is he is hiding, and it can be understood why he is often credited with mystical powers to the extent that this combines in the imaginations of enemy soldiers and plays havoc with their minds and morale.

This fear should be used to the maximum effect when deploying snipers, and indeed is the driving force in any good sniper doctrine. The sniper must always keep that knowledge of his power over his enemy in the back of his mind, and when selecting his target consider the effect it will have on the target's fellow soldiers. If the sniper believes that shooting another individual will affect the masses even more, then he should consider removing him first. For every operation the sniper must assess the situation and decide which targets are the most important and then prioritise them for engagement. As an example, if the sniper is observing a group of soldiers who appear to have no discernible officers or identifiable leaders, then the sniper must identify the man within the group who appears to be most respected by the rest. This can be done by watching them over a period of time and observing who does the most pointing or indicates tasks to the others, or who it is that the others appear to be trying to impress. This is more than likely to be the individual within the group to whom everyone else looks up and whom they think is indestructible. If

ABOVE: A sniper scans the area ahead of him for enemy activity. The sniper's partner, not too far away, will be providing cover while the search takes place.

BELOW: A British sniper takes aim from the flank of the enemy position. Apart from natural vegetation camouflage, he uses "trapped shadow" to conceal him from enemy observation.

ABOVE: The author, working out of the front of reconnaissance Land Rover, using Saab laser training simulators while playing "enemy" for a large joint services armoured exercise in Canada. He is "engaging" low flying helicopters. Because this is an exercise, and because he is an instructor on this occasion, he is not wearing a ghillie suit.

this man is taken out, the morale of the group can be seriously affected, if not destroyed.

Snipers can be deployed in all phases of war, in any weather, day or night and even in chemical environments. While the sniper may have the reputation of being the "lone wolf" or "maverick" of the battlefield, roaming around and indiscriminately killing at will, nothing could be further from the truth. The sniper is very closely monitored and has specific roles within the battle plan. He can be used: (a) to kill selected enemy personnel; (b) to engage valuable enemy equipment; (c) to greatly delay or disrupt a much larger force by engaging them at maximum range or from areas from which they do not expect to be attacked; (d) to gather "real time" information and report it back to give commanders exact times and locations of the enemy position or advance.

The main battlefield role of the sniper is to kill selected enemy personnel and/or destroy important equipment, and it is up to the sniper to decide who, or what, within the group that he can see, is the most important target. This can be:

- Officers or NCOs.
- Snipers.
- Exposed armoured vehicle crews.
- Crew-served weapons crews.
- Crews of support helicopters.
- Radio operators.
- Specialists such as minefield-clearing parties.
- Any exposed vulnerable equipment such as radios, optics, radar, fuel, vehicles or armoured vehicle sights and vision devices.

The human targets can be located and identified by various means, such as type of uniform, visible badges of rank, weapon or equipment carried, and reactions of others around them, such as saluting. Within some armies the officer corps are totally in command and are the only ones who have military skill and knowledge. In this scenario, to shoot the officer will cause a complete breakdown of military order and so seriously affect the enemy's ability to fight. In other armies it is the Non-Commissioned Officers that hold everything together within the ranks and so here they would be the priority targets.

The most dangerous weapon facing both the sniper and his fellow infantryman is undoubtedly the enemy sniper; he is therefore a very high priority target if known to be used by the enemy.

It is evident that a sniper is not capable of destroying a main battle tank, although he can however kill the crew, if exposed, and systematically destroy vision blocks and weapons-associated equipment such as laser sights, thermal sights and computer masts. This would force the remaining crew to batten down, restricting their view, and by removing valuable equipment reduce their effectiveness. The recent introduction of a laser training unit for the British Army sniper rifle means that for the first time snipers can now take part in large scale military exercises using laser-weapons-effect simulators. As a result, tank crews are starting to realise just how much of a threat snipers can be to them and their equipment.

Crew-served weapons, such as heavy machine guns, mobile missile systems, mortars, artillery, automatic grenade launchers and anti-aircraft weapons are all high priority targets for the sniper. The reason for this is that these weapons can do a lot of damage to friendly forces, so to remove the crew also removes the weapon from the battle. Anyone stupid enough to take over the weapon after the crew have been shot, will receive the same fate. It is amazing just how quick people can learn when there's a sniper about!

Helicopters are notoriously easy to disable or destroy. With armour-piercing incendiary ammunition, the sniper is more than capable of bringing down a hovering helicopter. Even with normal sniper ball ammunition, a helicopter can be disabled with a well-placed shot into its engine or rotor area.

Radio operators are essential to the command and control of a military unit and so to remove them and their radio with well-placed shots will cause confusion and loss of control to the enemy. Again, anyone else who picked up the radio would receive the same fate, making the radio a no-go area. Within this group of targets come "runners" or anyone who appears to be passing on any information, or who apparently has anything to do with the running of the unit. If the soldier responsible for the resupply of food, water or any form of equipment is identified then he is openly taken out. This not only lowers morale, but also makes people reluctant to take over his job, and in a very short time the operational effectiveness of the unit is affected.

Military specialists such as engineers, chemical troops, reconnaissance troops or radar specialists are all high-risk jobs if there is a sniper in the area, since to remove these men or women is to reduce the capabilities of the enemy and put him at a disadvantage.

In offensive operations where a sniper finds himself working against a dug-in or entrenched enemy he can very quickly reduce the morale and efficiency of the unit. By watching the enemy for a short period of time, the sniper can establish the position's routine. The things he will look for are the commanders, the resupply and feeding rosters, defences, the latrine, communications equipment, fuel stores and anything else that, if removed, would affect the enemy's efficiency and will to fight.

What would appear to be of little consequence to winning a battle can in fact be very important. As an example, by locating the latrine area the sniper can shoot a soldier who uses it, and this will have two effects. First, it will make the whole enemy position feel vulnerable; second, and more important, it will force the soldiers to defecate within their trenches, thereby reducing their freedom of movement, increasing their stress and lowering the hygiene and morale. Add to this the killing of soldiers who bring any new supplies or who try to remove any waste from the trenches, and this makes for very unhappy living and hence a reduced will to win.

Furthermore, a shot into any radio or other communications equipment position will reduce the effectiveness of the position and isolate the soldiers there, since anyone leaving or arriving to see why they cannot contact the position by radio could also get shot.

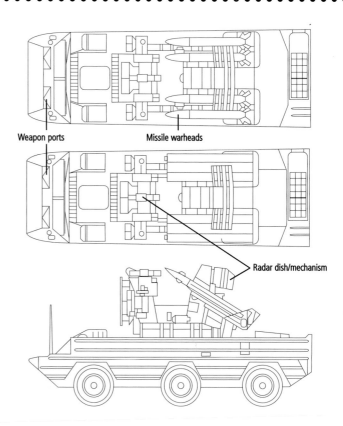

ABOVE: As well as shooting important human targets, snipers can be used to disrupt or destroy expensive and tactically valuable weapon systems, such as surface-to-air missile systems, by aiming at the known vulnerable and important points. The optics and guidance systems, plus communications equipment, are very susceptible to damage from .338 armour-piercing/arm our-piercing incendiary (AP/API) ammunition.

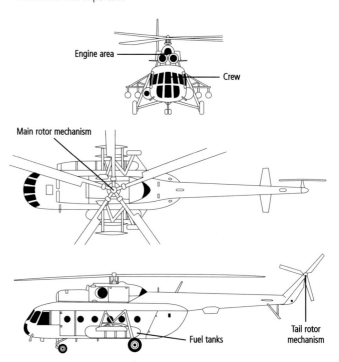

ABOVE: Support helicopters at the hover or while slow moving are also very easily engaged by snipers. Again the placing of an AP or API round, or even a standard ball round, into the fuel area of one of these aircraft is going to really ruin the crew's day. It is not just tank crews that are beginning to realise how much of a threat snipers can be to them.

All of these operations fall into the sniper's secondary role of harassing an enemy, and can cover a multitude of acts that in essence restrict or hinder and wear down the enemy.

A role that usually gets overlooked whenever people think of snipers is that of observation and reporting. This role is usually coupled to the sniper's main role of killing selected enemy personnel. It requires him to have the ability to read the overall battle plan of his commanders, and to know when to shoot and when to report in order to assist his commanders' plan and to not compromise it. Much of the sniper's time is spent observing the battlefield, looking for anything unusual that will lead him to his quarry. He is therefore the ideal man to assist and complement the reconnaissance troops.

Many reconnaissance soldiers resent the snipers as they feel that they infringe upon their task. They also feel that they can do a sniper's job and that therefore there is no real need for individual sniper-trained personnel. While there is no doubt that recce troops are very highly trained soldiers and that within their ranks they usually have sniper-qualified personnel, they are most definitely not trained to the extremely high standards that the sniper must reach. The sniper's test standards for such areas as observation and camouflage and concealment far outreach those of the recce troops, and should be used to complement and not replace the skills of the reconnaissance elements.

The sniper should work as an integral part of a unit's forward screen, be it in the defensive or offensive role, and as such be deployed to maximise the ability of both the sniper and his weapon system. Within that framework the sniper can use his powerful optics to search and scan for the enemy and report back to his high command any sightings or con-

ABOVE: Snipers use their superior concealment skills to maintain a watch on the enemy and to report his every move. If the tactical scenario will allow, they can also cause havoc by hitting and moving and not allowing the enemy to relax.

BELOW: A sniper section can be deployed into a blocking or ambush position, using their members' ability to engage from long range while remaining unseen. Here, a strategically placed Gurkha section awaits pre-designated targets.

ABOVE: A US Army M24 sniper rifle heavily camouflage-painted. It is generally considered to be a good weapon, with easy-to-use optics, that would cause great damage to an advancing enemy in the right hands.

tacts he may have, choosing whether the tactical scenario dictates that he should log and report, or engage and harass the enemy at extreme range.

EMPLOYMENT PRINCIPLES OF THE SNIPER

For the effective deployment of snipers the high command, from generals down to company commanders, must understand and trust the importance and skills of their snipers. If they do not, it is difficult for some of the more arrogant to ask (and admit there is something they do not know!), and also to accept that someone of such low rank may be that capable!

The pompous attitude of some army officers that was historically so instrumental in the resistance to sniping in the first place is still alive and causing just as many problems as it ever did. The snipers and some well-informed officers hold the British Army sniper system together, for example, but overall the system is very poor. While the standard of sniper is of the highest order, the investment in equipment is controlled by people with no sniper experience. Their understanding of and trust in the sniper's capabilities are poor. The training system is disjointed and open to corruption. The basic elements are without doubt the finest in the world, but the co-ordination is in need of a serious overhaul;

BELOW: Ever-watchful, and making optimum use of dead ground, their superior training and experience, a Gurkha sniper pair advance to make contact with the "enemy" during a British Army exercise in the Falklands.

at present the British high command pay only "lip service" to sniping, with men more interested in career enhancement papering over the cracks instead of rebuilding the system from ground level up.

This basic trust and understanding is essential if the snipers are to be used to the limits of their abilities and therefore deployed in such a way as to present a constant irritant to an enemy in both their forward and rear areas. The sniper is not a special forces soldier and should never be deployed as one, but he is a specialist and master of his trade, and will present a formidable opponent to any enemy force, including special forces. To ensure that the snipers are controlled and deployed to make the maximum use of their unique skills the following principles should be employed.

CONTROL AT THE HIGHEST LEVEL

Snipers are a brigade and not a company asset and therefore should ideally be controlled at that level or at the level of the highest command in the operation. Their use should be co-ordinated with all the other support elements such as mortars, artillery, heavy machine guns, recce and patrolling. The high level of training enables snipers to deploy as a pair or, more likely, as part of a combined reconnaissance and sniper screen or force. To enable them to do their job as efficiently as possible the snipers should be briefed by the highest level intelligence sources and should report directly back to that level, with their information being disseminated

down to local commander level as needed. This rarely happens; snipers usually become the local area commander's recce troops and therefore they are misused and wasted.

SELECTION OF SNIPER TASKS

Snipers should only be given tasks that require their particular skills. This is to ensure that the snipers are not deployed on a task that could have been done by other troops. This is not to imply that snipers think they are "special" or above certain jobs, but to emphasise the importance of ensuring that when their skills are needed, they are available and not tied up with unrelated tasks. In the past there have been such mistakes made as doubling up the sniper's task with that of nuclear, biological and chemical sentry. The thinking behind this has been that the sniper is forward of the friendly force's position, and so is the NBC sentry, so why not combine the task and get the sniper to do both? Well, the sniper is a very mobile soldier whose survival relies upon his being totally focused on the area around him and therefore he does not have the time to monitor NBC detectors or other NBC-related equipment. The general rule has to be not to give a job to a sniper that is within the capabilities of other available soldiers who are non-specialists.

THE TWO-MAN TEAM

The likelihood of a single sniper deploying on his own, in the "lone-wolf" type scenario, would be very rare indeed, although the snipers are all trained to do that should the need arise. The normal deployment is of the sniper pair. This consists of two men, both sniper qualified, who work as a team. The senior man, usually an NCO, is the primary sniper while the second team member is the spotter or observer.

BELOW: A sniper prepares his route out after receiving his orders to deploy into a harassing role. Each leg will be designed to put him at an advantage over his enemy, and will have taken into account enemy tactics and strengths.

The team will usually deploy with one sniper rifle and one close-protection weapon such as an M16 or M4/M203 combination to provide intimate fire support for the sniper pair should they be compromised and engaged by the enemy. It is common practice for the sniper to carry a sidearm of some form, usually his army-issue pistol, for his own close protection. While the pair is the normal deployment option, the task may require more than one sniper pair, so two pairs or even a whole sniper platoon may be deployed to carry out a sniper-related task such as ambush or area denial.

LOCAL PROTECTION AND BACK-UP

The sniper pair, not being a large fighting force and being very lightly armed will require the support of others if it runs into trouble. The sniper takes a long time to train and, while cost-effective when compared to the cost of a modern armoured fighting vehicle, he is just as valuable and hard to replace, and so it would make sense to provide him with some form of supporting fire should he need it.

The sniper should be controlled at the highest level, and also included in the overall fire plan and battle scenario; this will lock him into the arcs of any supporting weapons. Within this framework the sniper should be allocated some form of direct fire support that he can call on if he requires to extract himself from a firefight of some sort. This can take

ABOVE: Sniper pair moving in a circular route to maximise the cover of the longer grass and the colour that matches their suits. Moving across the darker grass would expose them.

BELOW: The closer to the enemy the pair get, the slower and lower they move, making the most of every fold in the ground. It is an exhausting way to travel, and they must be fit.

the form of artillery, mortars, ground attack aircraft, heavy machine guns or a platoon held in a supporting position. Whichever is allocated, it must be on priority call to the sniper and not on another task when he needs it, unless the tactical situation gives urgent priority to someone or something else.

ENDURANCE

It must be realised that the sniper pair cannot work indefinitely, and that the work they carry out is very demanding both mentally and physically. When they are deployed upon any task, the deploying commander must give careful consideration to the length of time the mission will last, the type of operation he expects the snipers to carry out, and the requirements in terms of manpower and resources they will need to succeed.

The snipers will be limited physically by the amount of equipment they can carry, and mentally by the time that they can remain fully alert. Any operation over twenty-four hours in duration will see a gradual decrease in the snipers' mental ability, as the effects of limited and broken sleep start to take effect. For operations over forty-eight hours in length, the commander should include relief in place for the sniper team from a second sniper team, so as to maintain the highest levels of observation and mental awareness.

The careful selection of personnel during the training phase of any sniper course will ensure that like-minded men are matched to work together at an early stage. This pairing should be further encouraged throughout training and operational deployments to foster a deep and trusting working relationship. This will lead to a pair who know each other's strong and weak areas and compensate accordingly to make the team a success. This system will also ensure that a team is deployed whose members, through understanding and trusting each other, can better cope with the emotional and mental strains of the long and dangerous operations and with the prolonged periods of isolation.

ABOVE: Contact! The sniper pair locates the enemy and starts to gather intelligence on his strengths, weaknesses and dispositions ready to relay to other snipers and his HQ.

BELOW: In a suitably concealed position, the sniper marks in red permanent pen the enemy locations ready to be passed on to his HQ or to call in indirect fire support.

RULES OF ENGAGEMENT

Any deployment of snipers must be done with very clear rules of engagement. To deploy them without these could lead either to the snipers not making full use of any advantage over the enemy they may have, or the complete compromise of the bigger plan because the snipers fired and indicated a military presence to an enemy that was unaware of one.

The rules of engagement may be a set of laid-down SOPs or may have been issued by a local area commander to suit his battle plan or requirements. For either to work they must be clear, unambiguous and not endanger the sniper pair by being too restrictive. To achieve the last point, a clear understanding of how snipers deploy and their limitations must be known to the issuing commander. The snipers must also have good communications to the issuing commander to facilitate the need for modification or change in the event that the tactical situation demands it.

COUNTER-SURVEILLANCE

The battlefield of today is covered with all manner of surveillance devices, and these are both active and passive. Snipers must be aware not only of their own role and position within the framework of the plan but also that of supporting friendly forces. To give themselves away may well lead to the discovery or compromise of other friendly troops' positions. The overall commander will issue a surveillance and target acquisition plan (STAP), and this will cover the rules for the use of both active and passive equipment. The snipers must adhere to this, but their own thermal signature and the concealment of it is their own problem.

TACTICAL EMPLOYMENT

There have been examples of how high standards of training of snipers have enabled them to achieve results that far outweigh their numbers, and these have been achieved in all areas of combat. While the sniper can have an effect on all phases of war, the success or failure depends as much on the way he is controlled and deployed as on his own ability and professionalism. Most military operations can benefit from the deployment of snipers, whether by using their shooting ability or their excellent observational skills, and their inclusion in any mission should be considered.

ABOVE: Snipers will work their way around their entire area of responsibility to gather as much information on the enemy as they can, and to probe for weak areas in his defences or formations.

BELOW: A sniper platoon prepares for deployment. Here these snipers will compare ideas, "de-conflict" over work areas and tie down their interlocking supporting arcs to ensure maximum success.

THE ADVANCE

Snipers have a very important role to play in the advance phase of battle. Their skills can give the overall commander as well as the local commanders a real advantage over the enemy. Snipers should be deployed well in advance of the main force so as to maximise the location of the enemy by them or recce troops. If the enemy position is already known, then snipers may be deployed behind the enemy lines to either hold the enemy or ambush likely enemy withdrawal routes, killing and harassing for as long as possible to inflict maximum damage and lessen his will to fight.

Alternatively, snipers can be held back with the main force in order to be available for speedy deployment to positions that will support any rapid attacks that may result from the advance. This type of deployment will allow them to locate suitable positions from which to dominate the enemy positions and/or likely lines of enemy withdrawal. The snipers will be targeting the enemy commanders (so as to destroy the command and control), the communications per-

sonnel and equipment (to prevent the enemy from calling for any reinforcements or indirect fire support), enemy snipers or hidden positions, and any heavy weapons and their crews that could inflict high casualty levels upon attacking friendly forces. The snipers may also be deployed in blocking or ambush situations to slow or stop any enemy reinforcements arriving before the enemy position has been taken by friendly forces.

To ensure that they are fully fit to be used for these types of operation, the snipers should not be used as extra riflemen while they are not on sniping tasks, regardless of the temptation to do so, or complaints from local commanders. Wherever possible, they should travel with the command group and be rested when not needed.

When snipers are to be deployed as a blocking or ambush force, the deployment of them behind enemy lines should be given careful thought and consideration, and they should be deployed only if the task warrants the risk. When considering such operations some areas need close attention. The time available and just how it is intended to get snipers into position is obviously the prime consideration. Here, time will dictate what is and what is not a viable option. If time is short, then deploying on foot and covertly stalking into position are out of the question. Other insertion options such as by helicopter or vehicle will carry with them penalties of

BELOW: A French sniper student pauses to chamber a round while advancing toward an "enemy" defensive location on an international joint forces training course. It is his FRF2 rifle that gives away his nationality even though he is wearing British pattern uniform.

noise and extra manpower, and may alert the enemy to the impending attack. Therefore, detailed planning will be driven, to some extent, by the factor of available time. In reality the tactical situation will again push commanders into a decision, but the deployment of snipers, who can dominate a large area and remove key threats with surgical rifle fire, will release other much-needed troops for the assault.

Snipers are also the obvious choice for the role of flank protection of the main advancing force, although how they would keep up within an armoured unit is a major consideration. One option would to be to provide them with light vehicles that they can easily conceal when required, such as motor cycles or 4x4 quads/ATVs (all-terrain vehicles). Indeed, during the Gulf War the British SAS used motorcycle outriders to provide flank protection to the Desert Patrol Vehicles (Land Rover gun ships) during their deployment behind Iraqi lines.

To use the snipers to the greatest advantage, the commander must allow them time to deploy and to locate suitable areas from which to observe and shoot at the enemy, otherwise their deployment will be wasted or they will be killed. This reaffirms the need for co-ordination at the highest level, since the deployment time of snipers will be a major factor in the overall commander's time appreciation and plan of action. He must also brief at the highest level on the sniper's tasks, deployment areas, radio call signs and recognition signals to ensure the advancing troops do not engage the snipers by mistake. Since all snipers are trained to call in and adjust indirect fire, such as mortar or artillery fire, their locating and reporting of a large body or concentration of enemy vehicles, equipment or personnel will facilitate the use of indirect support to maximise the damage inflicted upon the enemy. This will only happen, however, if it falls under the rules laid down in the commander's STAP plan.

ABOVE: A British sniper reverses his 4x4 quad vehicle into a small wood to conceal it before he closes with the enemy on foot. The "go-anywhere" quad is an excellent option for snipers working with armoured units, where the battle moves much quicker across the battlefield.

SNIPER TARGETS IN THE ADVANCE

- Command posts, OPs, snipers.
- Crew-served weapons – i.e. heavy machine guns/mortars.
- Defences and obstacles.
- Communication equipment.
- Likely reinforcement routes.

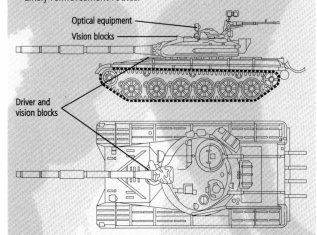

Optical equipment
Vision blocks
Driver and vision blocks

ABOVE: While snipers are unlikely actually to destroy a well-armoured tank, they can nevertheless hinder them by forcing exposed crews to batten down, thereby reducing their vision, or by firing at the tank's vision blocks and optics and by damaging secondary armaments with rifle fire.

OBSTACLES

Any advancing friendly force will inevitably encounter obstacles of some sort, be they natural or man-made, and will have to cross them in a tactical and defendable way. In this situation, snipers will be pushed out to positions that dominate the surrounding areas of land. In this way the snipers can afford early warning of an enemy's advance into the area and buy the commander time by engaging and slowing the enemy advance. This will enable the crossing to be completed or a defensive plan to be put into effect.

THE ATTACK

The role of snipers in the deliberate attack is very similar to that in the hasty attack during the advance. The main difference is the increased time factor afforded in the planning of a deliberate attack. Snipers can be deployed in some considerable advance of the main attacking force to locate and accurately report on the enemy dispositions while remaining unseen. They can continue to report up to the time of the attack commencing, or if the battle plan allows it they can engage and harass the enemy, thereby wearing him down, for a considerable time prior to the main assault.

On the assault itself, the snipers will engage priority targets with precision fire into enemy positions to ease the casualties in and workload on the attacking troops. They can also report on the progress of the battle to higher command and warn of any building counter-attack, or engage it and

BELOW: During the Gulf War campaign in 1991, snipers were able to deploy to within range of the large Iraqi defensive positions prior to the Coalition's major armoured advance, and thereby reduce enemy morale by constantly harassing them and affording them no rest.

slow its deployment, with either their own weapons or with indirect fire. One successful tactic that has been used to great effect before is to have the snipers identify crew-served weapon locations during the recce phase of the attack. On H hour (the start of the assault) the crews can all be taken out and replacement crews given the same attention, thereby keeping the heavy weapons out of the battle, and reducing the risk to the attacking soldiers quite considerably.

Before any sniper deployment, the positions and the direction of assault must be carefully considered and co-ordinated to avoid any friendly fire casualties. The correct

CHARACTERISTICS OF SNIPER FIRE BASE POSITIONS

- Good observation.
- Good concealment.
- Protection from fire/defendable.
- Good arcs of fire.
- Communications.
- Alternative positions if required.

SNIPER TASKS DURING THE ATTACK

- Kill key personnel prior to assault starting.
- Accurate fire into enemy positions.
- Destroy/disable crew-served weapons.
- Counter-sniping.
- Flank protection.
- Engage retreating/reinforcing enemy.
- Cover the friendly forces' reorganisation phase.

siting of the snipers will afford them good cover from enemy view and fire, and will allow them to engage the enemy, and thereby support the attack, for the complete battle without being obscured by the movement of friendly forces, and thus reducing their effectiveness. The snipers are not restricted to one position. Indeed, they may prepare and then occupy several positions during the attack, to ensure they play the most effective role they can and to keep up with the flow and forward momentum of the battle.

The normal procedure is for the snipers to be deployed off to a flank to cover an attack. But there is an alternative. In some circumstances the snipers may deploy with the attacking troops to provide intimate support and remove any hold-ups. This option provides the following advantages:

• Shorter ranges.
• Faster response time to requests for assistance.
• Good communications with assaulting troops.
• Good coverage of the enemy position being engaged, ensuring fire exactly where it's needed.

There are, as with all options, some disadvantages:

• The snipers become tied down and lose mobility.
• The snipers' ability to assist a wide section of the assault is reduced.
• The snipers burn more energy and need recovery time.
• The snipers' response time to secondary deployment is seriously affected.

BELOW: A French sniper pair works closely together to provide the shooter with a steady firing position. The pair is using the bush as a screen from enemy observation, although it would provide no cover from probing fire.

Overall, the deployment of snipers to assist in the attack of an enemy position will greatly reduce the risk to the assaulting troops, because of the snipers' ability to remove high-risk enemy assets from the equation. The ground, combined with the tactical situation and time available, will dictate the level at which the snipers can assist, and their inclusion must be carefully planned, to avoid casualties or restrictions in their effectiveness.

Snipers may also be used to confuse the enemy by delivering a decoy or feint attack. The reason for this could be to deceive the enemy into believing the attack is coming from another direction, thereby giving the actual assaulting troops time and cover to deploy unhindered to their intended start line. With the enemy's attention diverted, and possibly some of his major weaponry, the snipers can engage and hold the enemy in contact long enough for the real attack to be launched, to then engage priority targets in support of the attack.

THE REORGANISATION

This reorganisation phase of any assault is without doubt the most vulnerable for the attacking forces. This is because it is the first time since the start of the assault that the troops can tend wounded, secure prisoners, reorganise themselves and re-issue ammunition, so it tends to be a period of confusion. It is also the most likely time for the enemy to muster his forces and take back what has just been taken from him, since he will be well aware of the attacker's situation and recognise it as his best opportunity to be successful.

In this situation the hasty deployment of snipers, with their ability to hold up and seriously damage an enemy force from long range, will buy the local commander enough time to regain control of his force, issue quick orders, and consolidate his position. For this reason it is a very prudent commander who includes this option in his overall plan and orders.

SNIPER TASKS WITHIN THE DEFENSIVE BATTLE

With the advantage of a prepared position and time to plan, the sniper is without doubt at his most effective in the framework of the defensive battle. With the advantage of reconnaissance, and knowledge of the enemy's SOPs, the sniper can be placed in the most likely areas through which the enemy is expected to advance. The positioning and

ABOVE: Snipers training to engage multiple advancing targets at various ranges. In this situation, the snipers must prioritise the targets into an order of the biggest threat downward and engage them accordingly.

BELOW: A sniper section has a final briefing before breaking down into pairs to advance and engage the enemy from multiple directions. Note that while they confer, at least one maintains visual contact to remove the risk of surprise attack.

intended results of snipers can be constructed to achieve the desired results of the local commander, be it to delay the enemy or to channel him into a specific killing area. The control of snipers at the highest level is essential here since there will be an abundance of tasks for the snipers to become involved in, and so an order of priority for any tasks or targets must be made.

THE SCREEN

The deployment of a screen, or shield of carefully positioned snipers, is intended to ensure that no enemy can penetrate a given area of ground without the local commander's knowledge, and the snipers can be a very effective addition to its make-up. Within the overall plan of action for the screen, snipers can be used to limit enemy observation and deployment, and to delay, frustrate and engage the enemy at maximum ranges. The secondary sniper skills of observing and reporting can also be of vital importance.

Snipers should always be an integral part of the screen and can be used to dominate areas that would otherwise have taken many more troops. From their positions as part of the screen, snipers can use their superior optics and knowledge of concealment to locate and identify enemy reconnaissance elements and engage them with accurate long-range rifle fire. This action will force the early deployment of the enemy forces and will be both time-consuming and tiring for the enemy soldiers. To remove the enemy recce elements is to force the enemy to advance blind and with much more caution, enabling friendly force units to pick off selected personnel and equipment as the enemy advances.

Snipers can also be deployed to cover likely approach routes, natural or man-made obstacles and potential attack forming-up points. This will all have a detrimental effect on the enemy morale, command and control, and will to fight.

The enemy soldiers already know they are advancing into combat and potential death or injury, and so will be suffering from varying amounts of stress. To be engaged by an unseen enemy who allows them no vent for their fears, because they cannot shoot what they cannot see, and who has attacked them way before the point that they had come to accept would be the point where they started risking their lives plays havoc with their minds. And then to be engaged again by this invisible enemy, just when they thought he had gone, and to witness even more single-shot casualties, will of course deplete their already waning desire to fight.

Most soldiers mentally prepare themselves for battle, and pick a place on the ground or a time that they acknowledge will be the start of combat. To this end they convince themselves that in any area or time before that they are at low risk, and as such safe from attack. The forming-up point is one such area. This area is out of direct line of sight to the enemy and considered safe enough for final battle preparations, kit and ammunition issues, confirmation of attack plans and the shake out into final attack formations. Imagine then, the panic and confusion that will ensue if a sniper or snipers engage the enemy in this phase. The loss of men to single-shot wounds will create panic and confusion. And when the snipers feel that to remain would risk themselves being killed, they call in indirect fire support onto the enemy and withdraw to await the arrival of the enemy further along their route, ready to do it all again. This is all before the enemy has even seen the main focus of their attack.

This type of sniper tactic will more than likely be combined with the likes of mobile anti-armour units and mortar fire control parties in order to inflict the most damage upon the enemy. When these units withdraw, the snipers remain to use successive fall-back positions to maintain the pressure on the advancing enemy. The ability to see without being seen, and to kill without being killed, is the sniper's main strength, and his key to mental domination of his enemy. In this way the snipers can keep a much stronger force off balance and fighting to just maintain some form of command and control. It is also possible to use the snipers to lead the enemy into the wrong area by giving him the false impression of a main defensive position, when in fact the real defensive location is elsewhere. In this way, the enemy can be successfully delayed or led into a killing area of the local commanders' choosing.

ABOVE: A commander indicates the area he wishes snipers to operate in and control. The snipers will remain in radio contact.

BELOW: A British sniper adopts the laid back position to engage a long-range target. In war, he will constantly harass the enemy.

MAIN DEFENSIVE POSITION TASKS

When the screen has achieved its mission it will move back to occupy its main defence positions, and the enemy can be expected to start to probe for positions and the overall disposition of the defending force. During this phase the snipers can again be deployed to the flanks and likely approach routes to deny and disrupt the enemy's movements. In this scenario the snipers will be working from the previously sited and constructed hides, often with assistance from the units they are supporting or located near. These sites will enable them to use the ground to the maximum advantage. They may be on forward slopes, where the snipers will be ideally located to provide long-range observation and fire, or on the flanks or depth positions where the snipers may use their long-range weaponry to greatest effect. The co-ordination of the snipers' tasks will again be controlled at the highest level, to ensure the correct prioritising of targets and the co-ordination of sniper ambushes and volley fire.

One of the main reasons for locating the snipers away from the main positions is to ensure that they can engage the enemy throughout the enemy attack, usually from a right-angle position on the flanks, and also to minimise the effects on the snipers of artillery and mortar fire, which will obviously be used against the main position in an effort to suppress the defender's weaponry. In this way the snipers can be used to help break up the enemy attack when the main defence position is being subjected to heavy indirect fire, and so reduce the chances of the enemy forces following a creeping barrage on to the main position.

The snipers can also be used to support any counter-attacks by friendly forces by engaging the enemy with precision rifle fire. If it is found that the snipers' main positions do not allow for the support of any counter-attack, then the snipers must be prepared to move rapidly into positions that will enable them to provide the support requested. If movement is required then the counter-attacking commander must allow time for the snipers to redeploy, into positions that will enable them to engage the enemy location or to isolate it and prevent the enemy from reinforcing it once the counter-attack has started.

RELIEF OPERATIONS

Within the scenario of defence comes the relief operation. When troops are in a combat situation for any length of time, their combat effectiveness starts to deteriorate and so some form of change around of units must take place. This is called a "relief in place" and snipers can provide valuable assistance in its smooth running. A defensive position is very vulnerable while any relief takes place, and to be attacked at this stage could cause massive confusion and a loss of control. This in turn could lead to heavy casualties or the loss of the position, and so the security and early warning of any enemy movement is vitally important. Any snipers on the position to be relieved should be deployed to forward and flank positions to cover any likely enemy approach routes, using their optics and superior observation and concealment skills to watch for any enemy activity. More importantly, the snipers can buy the defensive position time by engaging and delaying the enemy.

On the successful completion of the relief, the deployed snipers will withdraw back onto the main position. It is

SNIPER TARGETS IN THE ATTACKING FORCE

- Commanders.
- Armoured vehicle crews.
- Crew-served weapon crews.
- Snipers/sharpshooters.
- Mortar/artillery-directing personnel.
- Radio operators.
- Specialists (engineers, etc.)
- Machine gunners.

SNIPER TASKS IN THE SCREEN

- Limit enemy observation.
- Location and destruction of enemy recce elements.
- Real-time reporting of enemy movements and strengths.
- Harass, disrupt and delay the enemy force.
- Assist in any deception plans.

SNIPER TASKS IN THE DEFENSIVE POSITION

- Dominate enemy approaches to main position.
- Counter-sniping.
- Kill selected enemy during the assault.
- Support any friendly force counter-attacks.
- Act as additional indirect fire OP.

essential that the out-going snipers have a face-to-face brief with the snipers of the relief force to ensure that any relevant information is passed over – such as enemy activity, likely tactics and approaches, and any sketches or air photos of the area of tactical responsibility. This will ensure the continuity of the sniper coverage and intelligence-gathering reports that will have already been collated.

PATROLLING

The domination of no-man's-land, or the area between two opposing forces, is essential to maintaining the upper hand over the enemy. Patrolling of these areas must be established irrespective of the type of terrain, be it open countryside or urban, and the sniper's skills at moving and dominating large areas may well be called into use. The type of task that would fall to the sniper is to carry out covert "scouting" patrols to look for any signs, no matter how small, of the enemy and indications of his intentions. The unit's reconnaissance troops would also be deployed, but their primary function is to move stealthily around the battlefield in order to locate the main enemy force.

It stands to reason therefore that the enemy will also have deployed his own recce troops and these soldiers will be using their skills to remain undetected. Here the superior concealment and observation skills of the snipers will come into play. Snipers are the ideal soldiers to study the terrain and assess the most likely routes that the enemy recce troops will take, bearing in mind all the available covered approaches and dead ground.

Armed with this knowledge, the snipers can be deployed into mobile stalks of designated areas of responsibility, or into hide locations over-watching the likely approach routes. The appreciation of the situation will also have taken into account the method of movement the enemy is using – either foot or vehicle – and the sniper will plan accordingly with such assets as fire support against an armoured or mechanised enemy, if available, and heavy machine guns against an enemy on foot. Remember, while the snipers can inflict heavy casualties on an unprepared enemy, artillery and machine guns can inflict even more; therefore, once the snipers have fixed the enemy's position and are in contact, they will always call in any available indirect support that in order to inflict the maximum damage on the enemy.

ABOVE: A British sniper advances slowly along the wood line, reducing the likelihood of his being seen by using the trees as his backdrop. He must proceed with caution, not knowing if the enemy lays beyond the thicket.

ABOVE AND BELOW: A sniper's rule: never assume. These photos show how easily he could be caught out by cutting corners or assuming the ground ahead is clear. Above, there appears to be no enemy for miles. The photo below was taken after advancing only 100 feet (30m) and proves that dead ground can work against him if he gets lazy!

Other patrolling tasks that snipers may be called upon to carry out are those where a close target recce has a particularly hard stalk in order to get close enough to collect the necessary information. Snipers may also be used to support the unit's reconnaissance troops by providing a fire support base overlooking the target if the close recce soldiers get into trouble.

Snipers are also used to man ambush sites; these situations can be either complete sniper ambushes, where a sniper screen ambushes a wide area or major natural obstacle, or where the snipers are deployed into cut-off positions to ensure no-one escapes the killing area. If the enemy to be ambushed is armoured or vehicle mounted, then the crews – and in particular the drivers – will become priority targets for the snipers. By engaging the leading and last vehicles first, the snipers or other troops can effectively block the enemy inside the killing area and inflict high casualties.

THE SNIPER IN THE URBAN ROLE

The world becomes more urban with every passing day, and so it is highly likely that snipers will be deployed into urban areas. Indeed, this has already happened in recent years with US Marine Corps snipers deploying in both Beirut and Mogadishu, and more extensively the British snipers operating in Northern Ireland.

The deployment of snipers into urbanised areas will take one of two forms, either all-out war or on internal security duties, and each has its own set of rules.

In general armed conflict, the destruction and damage to an urban area is enormous, as witnessed recently in the Balkans and Chechnya, and this will lend itself to the operating styles of the sniper. The options open to the sniper are many and varied and can include sitting in a rural area and engaging targets inside a town, sitting in the town and engaging targets outside the town, or using the destruction and confusion to exploit the tactical situation and the short-

SNIPER TASKS IN URBAN WARFARE

- Counter-sniping.
- Domination of routes and obstacles.
- Flank and rear protection/observation.
- Deny enemy movement.
- Engagement of opportunity targets.
- Indirect fire control.
- Supporting attacks and counter-attacks.
- Harass and disrupt the enemy.

ABOVE: British sniper rifle in a weapon cover made in the author's urban design.

range opportunities the urban area offers. Whichever option, or combination of options, the sniper chooses, he can have a major effect on the enemy's ability to move and fight. The enemy cannot afford to ignore a sniper once he has made contact, and to remove him is both time-consuming and manpower intensive.

The command and control of snipers is very difficult in the urban arena and will take thought and imagination in order to use them to the limits of their abilities. Such tasks as the domination of access routes through the rubble or defences, or the covering of obstacles to slow down and harass an enemy are ideal for snipers. The snipers must still be given clear rules of engagement that are built around the

BELOW: A British Army sniper returns to camp after a border patrol in Northern Ireland. Snipers can be a very useful tool in the internal security role and are deployed more frequently than people would believe.

local or area commander's concept of operations, and which also allow enough freedom of movement to protect the snipers and enough restraint to prevent the snipers from compromising themselves by engaging anything that moves.

While the fighting of an urban battle is very difficult, at least the enemy is well defined and usually in a uniform. However, the battle against the terrorist in an internal-security-type operation presents the sniper with a completely different set of problems. In this area the limitations are the law and the imagination, with a touch of the "who dares wins' attitude. The major problem that snipers face in this area is that of remaining unseen, and while anything in rural areas is the sniper's "bread and butter" the skills required to work among an alien civilian public are completely different.

In this scenario snipers will be given extremely tight and clear orders and rules of engagement, and to break them could lead to a courtroom appearance and possibly a prison sentence. The planning phase of any such operation is very detailed and is scrutinised at every stage. Snipers may be deployed overtly as a part of a routine patrol with the intention of letting the snipers' presence be known to the local terrorists, using the natural fear of snipers to discourage any terrorist activity. More often, however, snipers will be deployed covertly to occupy a hide.

Once a requirement for a sniper's deployment has been identified, the hunt starts for a suitable hide and deployment option. The task may be to cover a normal, overt patrol by friendly forces through a known terrorist area of operations. The aim would be to engage any terrorist gunmen who arrive, ambushing a specific area of interest or intelligence-gathering. Each one will be approached with an open mind and imagination.

ABOVE: One of the many deployment options available to snipers operating in the anti-terrorist role is that of the security force armoured vehicles that can drop them off and pick them up again in remote locations. Different vehicles would likely be used in general warfare situations.

The first task is to locate the hide position. This will be done with the aid of maps, air photos, intelligence and patrol reports from the area, and by visual reconnaissance. The location, once selected, will be the subject of close scrutiny, but meanwhile ensuring that nothing is done to draw attention to the place. There are various methods of viewing the location. One is to join a normal overt patrol and walk past it as part of the patrol route. Another is to conduct a walk-past wearing civilian clothing, with the sniper ensuring that he blends in with the neighbourhood. The latter method is extremely dangerous and should be carried out only by experienced snipers. A third method is the drive-past. This involves driving past the chosen hide location in order to study it, but this is limited in effect since the speed of the vehicle constrains the amount that can be seen, and to drive by more than once is to court compromise. The option to use close-circuit cameras or to fly-by in a helicopter can also to be considered and, if available, should be used.

With the information gathered on the daylight walk-past, a night-time close-target recce is planned. This will take the form of the sniper pair deploying either alone covertly or as part of an overt patrol, using the darkness and shadows to drop off the patrol at a given point without being noticed. Once away from the patrol, the snipers gain entry to their selected location in order to check its suitability for the task. The location can be anything from an occupied building to

ABOVE: A typical scene in an urban anti-terrorist operation – a city centre with potentially a multitude of innocent civilians who could be caught up in a bad situation. This is ideal ground for the sniper with his well-practised ability to hit the right person and not the uninvolved.

a pile of rubbish, and its selection depends on its suitability and the likelihood of compromise.

Once the snipers have completed their recce, including the taking of infrared photos for planning purposes, they will call for the patrol to return to cover their extraction, and the next phase can begin.

The planning for the actual operation has to be very detailed, since the snipers will be working away from immediate support, and their safety will depend heavily on remaining undiscovered. Some of the considerations for the snipers are as follows:

COVERT ENTRY:
- Doors – type of door, hinges, framework.
- Windows – type, glass, locks.
- Locks – type, replacements, pickable.
- Natural openings – holes in roof, walls, etc.
- Forced entry – noisy, ground sign, takes practice.

APERTURE:
- Brickwork – will require a drill.
- Glass – if breaking will draw attention; consider replacing with a thin plastic, or allow for through-glass shot.
- Roof space – may be a need to lift tiles or the corner of the roof using bottle jacks.

FALSE WALL OR DROP:
- Colour.
- Must reach from ceiling to floor.
- Must reach wall to wall.
- Identification of material best suited to task.

Due to the close proximity of the civilian population and their probable sympathies to the terrorist cause, a strict routine must be adhered to if the snipers are to avoid compromise. The routine must become a drill, with each man monitoring the other to ensure both remain alert and do not start to cut corners when tired. The minimum of equipment will be unpacked to facilitate a hasty exit if required, and extra close-protection weapons will be taken in as well as the sniper rifle. These may take the form of shotguns, machine guns, pistols or any other weapon considered suitable to the task that is available.

In some instances there may be a requirement to have the sniper weapon "delivered" after entry has been gained. In this instance two other snipers will adopt any suitable disguise in order not to draw attention to themselves, and will deliver the weapon to the hide. Disguise may take the form of refuse collectors, who leave more than they collect, or delivery/repair men who conceal the weapon in the delivered goods.

The general rule for urban covert insertion is that there is no rule, and it is dependent upon the snipers' imagination and nerve. Snipers will watch the daily pattern of life around the target and identify an option that will not draw attention to their movements. If they fear compromise, they will extract, since a terrorist unit will come in after them and a sniper pair will remain vulnerable as their back-up force will be at least minutes away. That can be long enough to lose two men.

WITHDRAWAL OPERATIONS

One famous World War II American general once said, "I'm not retreating, I'm just fighting in a different direction!" For many reasons it may be necessary to conduct a withdrawal. An example of modern day withdrawal is the short-term UN-type operation where forces go into a country for a short period only to restore peace, and then conduct a military withdrawal. Another reason for withdrawal is the need to fall into line with flanking units as part of an overall brigade position. Snipers can again assist with the security and early warning of the moving unit. The snipers, who should already be deployed, can remain in location to provide the unit with observation on the likely enemy approach routes. If necessary, and if the unit is withdrawing under contact with the enemy, then the snipers can provide precision fire in support of the friendly unit. This will not only assist the unit in breaking free of the enemy, but will also increase the troops' morale, since troops do not generally like the idea of withdrawing and so morale takes a dive. To hear and know that the enemy is taking punishment from the unit's own snipers will give them a boost. The snipers can then use their skill of moving unseen across the battlefield to extract themselves and rejoin their unit in its new area.

The snipers would reduce the enemy's reconnaissance ability by shooting their recce troops and slow the advance.

They would then engage targets that have been selected to cause the most damage and confusion to the enemy advance, and then fall back to a second pre-sited position and await the enemy, so as to start the process again. The snipers would work in conjunction with a small delaying force, who would also operate from previously prepared fallback positions. Good communications between them is essential to ensure the co-ordinated movement of the force, and to reduce the risk of "blue on blue" contacts – that is, the engaging of friendly troops by mistake.

The maximum use of the available ground is essential in this type of operation and any natural obstacles should be

SNIPER TASKS IN THE WITHDRAWAL

- Harass the enemy and inflict casualties.
- Observe and report enemy activity.
- Indirect fire control.
- Assist the main force to break contact

BELOW: During force withdrawal, a sniper pair watches and waits for any signs of the enemy while their comrades pull back under their cover. With their ability to hit the enemy from long range, the snipers can buy the withdrawing troops a considerable amount of time.

ABOVE: In general force withdrawal operations the snipers can remain and hold large areas of ground until the main force has successfully broken free and clear of enemy contact. They can then return under their own power to pre-arranged pick-up or link-up points.

included in the battle plan. To cover these with fire will not only seriously delay an enemy advance, but will inflict heavy casualties as well. The chances of discovering a sniper's location while trying to cross an obstacle are very low, and to try and force him or them out of the area with heavy weapons is both costly on supply lines, and on time – the one thing that any commander never has enough of in combat. The snipers have the ability to both waste the enemy commander's time and, more importantly, buy his own commander time.

In any withdraw operation, the snipers' actions and movements need to be very closely planned to co-ordinate with either the delaying force or the intermediate force, whichever command they come under. This not only reduces the risk of blue on blue situations, but ensures that the snipers fall back when they are supposed to and don't get over-run and lost to the enemy. If the snipers are to link up with the force whose command they come under, for either further operations or transport out of the area, then this action must be well planned and ideally rehearsed.

OPERATIONS OTHER THAN WAR

Today the most likely operational deployment a sniper is going to find himself in is one of low intensity. Conflicts such as Bosnia, Mogadishu, Kosovo and Sierra Leone are all recent examples of military action involving loss of life, but which are not all-out war situations, and snipers have been deployed in these and countless other similar instances. Sometimes they are up against a uniformed enemy, and sometimes they are faced with an enemy that not only is hard to identify, but also can contain both women and children.

These types of operations put the snipers under even more stress than is usual, and the importance of careful selection of the right men for the job in the selection and training stage become more apparent. Having in his cross-hairs a woman or young child toting an assault rifle and about to engage friendly forces is difficult to handle for most soldiers, and the decision to fire can cause deep after-thoughts. The decision has already been made for the sniper by his government and his commander, since they will have thought through and dictated the sniper's rules of engagement. If the woman or child has appeared in the sniper's reticule then they would already have come under those rules, or the sniper would not have aimed at them in the first place – and they *will* be shot. This is the scenario that can

ABOVE AND BELOW: When deploying in civilian vehicles and clothing during operations in urban settings, snipers must be able to deploy and fight with their back-up weapon, the pistol. Here, British snipers train with live ammunition to deploy from an urban ambush scenario.

face the sniper engaged on counter-insurgency operations, and the tactics and rules are far more flexible and politically driven.

In this type of operation it is likely that snipers will spend most of their time utilising their observation skills and gathering intelligence, while always maintaining their ability to remove a target with surgical precision. Whereas the sniper has always been considered a dark entity akin to an assassin, we are now in an era where, for the first time in his history, the sniper is a good thing and highly prized. The reason for this is that everything the military, and hence the government, does is watched on the world's television screens. There has not been a military operation in the last thirty years that has not been accompanied by the world's media, who are broadcasting the details before the troops involved have written their after-action reports.

The civilian world does not fully appreciate that war and combat of any type are not pretty, and that lives get lost. While it is laudable to call for talks and not combat, there is always going to be a need to enforce peace and freedom where there are those who try to take them away, and no matter how well it is dressed it up, combat is a messy and dangerous business. The world's media, who make money under the banner of "the people have a right to know", and the "tree hugging" protestors combine to make a very powerful rod with which to beat any government. For a government to ignore them is to risk to lose an election. To this end governments try to present the military as a user-friendly, politically correct organisation – but try as they may, it is not always possible, since after all, the military are in the business of killing, however reluctantly.

As a result of all this political interference the military usually find themselves working with their hands tied, where the enemy has an advantage. Such phrases as "collateral damage" are being bandied about. Most soldiers do not wish to destroy property or take life, but all realise that every now and again it is, unfortunately, a necessity. To save lives it usually pays to go in hard and fast. The recent British

ABOVE: This probably looks like an ordinary delivery van to most people, but in fact it could represent a drop-off vehicle, OP or firing position to a sniper in the internal security role. A sniper learns never to close his mind to different possibilities or suggestions, in attack or defence.

assault in Sierra Leone, to rescue troops from the "West Side Boys", stands as a perfect example. But had that action been on the streets of Belfast the world's press would have been singing a completely different tune. Oddly enough, against this background of political correctness and restriction, one type of soldier has emerged as acceptable – the sniper.

As unlikely as it would seem, the sniper has become the commander's choice of weapon in many such situations, such he has the ability to remove a gunman or other terrorist without hitting innocent civilians, or causing damage to property. Add a suppressed weapon to that equation, and the target is removed without the associated panicking crowd, running in all directions, giving a much worse image of the situation than is necessary.

In this politically and militarily dangerous theatre the sniper can be used in many ways. In areas where company-sized groups have enhanced freedom of action, snipers may well be placed under their command as opposed to being under the direct command of the battalion. In this scenario snipers may be used to covertly deploy into ambush position to deny insurgents access to the local population, or in known areas of insurgent activity. They may be used for the defence of key areas or installations known to be enemy targets, or deployed in support of cordon and search operations in areas that are "cordoned off". In cordon operations, the troops are at their most vulnerable on the insertion and extraction phase, so the early covert deployment of the snipers is ideal to provide the cordon troops with security from surprise attack or ambush.

The method of deploying the sniper screen will depend upon the type of conflict and the terrain. Options for the deployment include air delivery, by parachute or helicopter, or by foot or vehicle. Military vehicles attract attention and so to covertly deploy the snipers it may be necessary to use a civilian-type vehicle, such as a small truck or car and horse box. At the drop-off point the vehicle commander gets out and, perhaps, while pretending to urinate, checks the area both visually, to the limit of his night vision, and for any noise indications of someone being in the area. If there is, he simply gets back in and the vehicle is driven to an alternative drop off. If the area is clear he quietly opens the side door and the snipers melt into the night. The system can be used with a chase vehicle providing back-up a few minutes behind the drop-off vehicle, in case of ambush or chance contact.

At the end of the cordon operation, the snipers can remain in place and provide the extracting force with security, and be extracted themselves in the same way as they deployed.

SNIPER/MARKSMAN TASKS IN CIVILIAN AREAS

There are clear areas of everyday life where snipers, or more likely marksmen, have a role to play. Such areas cover armed assistance against crime, the protection of VIPs, counter-sniping or the protection of emergency crews in

times of civil disorder. In these circumstances, police marksmen, and not the military, would deploy in most countries. Certainly within the UK, the military would deploy snipers on to the streets only in extreme circumstances, although the situation in Northern Ireland is different and snipers are routinely deployed there. The tactics for deployment of police marksmen is very similar to those for the military sniper, and while he does not face the same rigours and dangers of the military sniper, the police marksman is an exceptional shot and every bit as professional.

NIGHT OPERATIONS

The closing of the day used to be an eagerly awaited time for forces involved in combat, especially to the losing side, since this brought with it a cessation in hostilities and a time to rest and recuperate, with the added possibility of a change in fortunes come the following morning. This break no

BELOW: The enemy never sleeps, and nor do snipers. With the multitude of night optics available, the sniper is just as deadly at night as he is in the day. Here, French snipers train on the range at night (their positions being illuminated and revealed only by the camera flash).

longer exists. The night is just as deadly as the day. Today's armies fight a 24-hour battle and snipers are just as effective at night as they are during the day, dependent upon the level of their training and the quality of their surveillance devices.

With the constant advances in night optics, the night-time is also becoming as dangerous to snipers as the day, and they have to pay as much attention to their camouflage and concealment during darkness as at any other time.

The roles a sniper will carry out at night differ only marginally from those he carries out in the day battle, with a reduction in range and a more cautious approach being two of the primary changes to his operational tactics. The concealment of his weapon report and muzzle flash is also a major added concern for the sniper at night, and needs to be carefully considered with each shot.

The main threats to the sniper at night are the variety of surveillance devices, either hand-held or static, that are readily available to today's soldiers. Image intensifiers, of various generations, are the most common type of night viewing optic on the battlefield and are usually issued down to section level and therefore pose a considerable threat to the sniper. These passive devices are harder to locate, but are visible when using another intensifier since they show up as a torch-like glow when viewed from the front, and if

located can be used as an aiming mark for the sniper's shot.

Thermal optics have already been mentioned and obviously pose quite a considerable threat to the sniper, but with knowledge of the operational and technical restrictions of such optics the sniper can survive on the thermal battlefield.

Infrared optics are less common nowadays since they work on an active principle and are therefore easily located by the sniper. He can use this readily available visible source not only to pinpoint the enemy's location, but also to also give himself an aiming mark.

One of the increasingly popular methods of monitoring areas of today is the use of man-portable radar. These systems are increasing in their proliferation and snipers would be well advised to become familiar with their operation and restrictions. Having worked with and against them, I can assure you that they can be bypassed. The relative experience of the operator will play a large part in the equipment's effectiveness.

Enemy patrols, both mobile and standing patrols, pose a threat to the sniper since his vision is restricted at night and he becomes more dependent upon his sense of hearing for his protection. The use of frequent listening stops is essential if the sniper is to survive the night stalk. Even the most disciplined troops will make some form of noise at night, be it human or human-related, such as equipment rubbing together or recognisable noises that the sniper has heard many times before. While not loud, they can be determined as definitely man-made and military in their origin. The sniper can avoid unwanted contact with the enemy by utilising his powers of hearing at night.

BELOW: A British sniper pair carrying out a daylight reconnaissance of their area of operations with a thermal optic. With these devices the sniper is becoming even more of a menace today, and can stalk the battlefield at night as well as in the day, to harass or report on the enemy's movements.

LEFT: With the daylight reconnaissance complete, the snipers deploy to their jump-off position just prior to last light. Here, the navigator pauses for a map check, while in the background his partner keeps watch to ensure they are not surprised by enemy action.

The extra problems that face the sniper at night will have the main effect of slowing him down in all that he does, and any planning of sniper tasking should take this into consideration. The act of navigation and route selection is much harder at night and, as has already been mentioned, the chances of being seen at night are just as great as they are in daylight, so the sniper must plan and move with extreme caution.

Target identification at night is also more difficult for the sniper, and he will almost definitely identify targets by what they are doing or the equipment they are carrying. The ranges that the sniper engages from will also be reduced, but this decrease will be directly related to the experience of the sniper and the standard of his optical night sights. With the latest generation of equipment, ranges of 550 yards (500m) are well within the capability of the sniper.

An essential factor and one that is sometimes overlooked is that of friendly force locations and their knowledge of the sniper's deployment and entry point to their position upon completion of his task. The last thing a sniper needs is to be engaged by his own troops because there has been a breakdown in communications and his impending arrival has not been passed down to the front line troops.

Snipers need sleep too, and to expect to be able to deploy them during the day and then at night as well, is risking their loss. Sniping is by nature a very physically and mentally draining task, and so care must be taken to ensure that snipers are well rested between deployments.

NUCLEAR, BIOLOGICAL AND CHEMICAL CONDITIONS

The sniper must be able to work in any weather and under any condition, and this includes NBC warfare. The British Army relies upon its detection and protective systems to allow its troops to fight in contaminated areas, and its snipers have to pass shooting tests in respirators in order to qualify. The sniper's roles in all phases of war do not change because of chemical contamination, but he does have to be aware of the extra limitations this type of threat poses.

When working ahead of the main force, snipers may not receive warning of chemical attack or contaminated areas, so they have to be extra vigilant to the threat in order not to be fatally caught out. They must also pay extra attention to the condition of their suits as they crawl across the battlefield and carry spares in case of damage. The threat of working in a chemical environment is a very real one, introducing many problems and restrictions. Nevertheless, the sniper is still expected to fulfil his task and so must train for such operations, ensuring that he is as prepared as he can be for such a demanding area of warfare.

SNIPER INSERTION METHODS

The traditional method of inserting snipers is having one or two men stalking slowly and over a short distance. While this is obviously still relevant, today's sniper pairs rarely work autonomously and often need insertion methods that

can cover a wide variety of terrain's and scenarios. With the many tactical options available for the employment of today's snipers, a commander may find himself with the need to push his teams several miles forward very quickly. In this scenario, the more options available to him, the more detailed and flexible his plan can become, giving it a much higher chance of success.

Very few units outside the special forces have many methods of transportation for the insertion of snipers. Indeed, few even spend time exploring the various options. But there are several ways of putting the sniper pair or section onto the battlefield – even if many officers who are not sniper-trained consider them "cowboy". And if a seemingly "James Bond-ish" option appropriate to the tack is dismissed by a senior officer and therefore cannot be used, the mission may have failed before it has even started.

The key to keeping the enemy guessing and your plans both flexible and unpredictable is to never discount anything before giving it a fair chance, no matter how unlikely it may appear at first. To discount an option just because it is unconventional and "not the way we do things around here" is foolish and asking for trouble. The fewer choices the planner allows himself the quicker he becomes predictable to the enemy, and the quicker his men die.

LAND OPTIONS

FOOT

The option of deploying on foot is the method that is the most commonly used. If the distance is not too great and if time permits, then it allows the sniper to select the most appropriate route to and from the target. It also provides the quietest option, greatly reducing the chances of early compromise. To deploy on foot requires the sniper to plan in

ABOVE: Recce troops can deploy forward and carry snipers to a suitable area, and liaise with them to undertake the extraction.

BELOW: As has ever been the case, the most obvious and often used deployment option for the sniper is the "mark one boot"!

great detail if he is to survive as he is closing with the enemy with little, and in some cases no, support. The sniper must make maximum use of maps, air photographs, previous patrol reports and recent local knowledge of the area from either military sources, who have operated in there, or from local civilians – taking great care not to compromise the mission in the process. The more detailed knowledge the sniper has to plan from, the better equipped he is to beat the enemy. By detailed planning the sniper can select a route than makes the most of available cover, both from enemy view and fire, and also taking note of any natural or man-made distractions that may mask his movement, such as fast flowing rivers or industrial areas.

MotorCycles

Under certain conditions the sniper will need to move large distances in a short time and will need a method of transport suitable to the task. One such method could be the motor cycle. Various military units throughout the world already use motorbikes to move around the battlefield or to the flank of friendly forces – so why not the sniper? This is not a new concept and has already been used to deploy sniper pairs both to the flanks and forward of larger formations. But motorbikes can only be used to get the snipers into the operational area before being cached, with the snipers continuing on foot. In the planning stage snipers must take into account the extra noise the bikes will make and therefore, in the map/air photo-study phase, should be looking for naturally covered routes and areas that will provide noise suppression, such as gullies or dead ground. In such areas as desert or the open plains of Africa, motorbikes can provide the extra range for snipers to be used to their maximum advantage, giving them the ability to move independent of

the main force, either to a flank or forward, and remain an effective option for commanders to use with both mechanised and armoured forces.

Quads and ATVs

Like the motorbike, the quad is a very effective way of moving small groups of men around the battlefield. Its main advantage over the bike is the fact that it is capable of carrying not only the sniper but all the stores and equipment he needs to be operational for several days. With many different types of quad on the market, it would not be difficult to select the one most suitable for individual unit or needs. Again some units have had the foresight to test these machines but usually in the resupply role or to carry support weapons, and not for the operational deployment of the sniper pair or screen. This would appear to be an amazing oversight.

Armoured Personnel Carriers

Many commanders consider the sniper to be ineffective in the armoured battle. This is not so. The only thing that will affect his usefulness is the inability to keep up with the battle, so if time and consideration are given to this problem, the sniper is just as effective as in any other phase of war. While lack of mobility in defence is not too much of a dilemma for the sniper, in the advance or transitional phase it most definitely is, so the problem needs to be addressed. As well as using bikes or quads, snipers can be moved for-

BELOW: 4x4 quad vehicles are a very good transport options for snipers. They are small, reliable and easily concealed, and when ridden correctly can prove very difficult to locate. Several British units have conducted successful trials with these vehicles, including the Army sniper school.

ABOVE: A revealing comparison between the British Army's Warrior IFV and a 4x4 quad vehicle. The latter has been loaded with a sniper's

deployment needs for a full five days' operation. One such vehicle can deploy a sniper pair and all their kit across almost any terrain.

snipers are the obvious choice to pre-deploy and to provide the extraction force as they can move to a prearranged helicopter pick-up point on foot, after the main force has extracted, using their ability to move unseen to avoid contact with enemy units en route.

ward by armoured vehicle under escort of the recce troops, or as part of a larger recce element, and covertly dropped off. Then they can move forward on foot or keep an area under observation as part of a larger recce/sniper screen, providing the recce troops with accurate supporting fire if needed while remaining unseen. With such weapons available as Barrett's .50 calibre anti-materiel rifle and the Accuracy International .338 Super Magnum with ammunition types including armoured piercing and armoured piercing incendiary, the sniper is more than capable of causing damage to enemy armoured units, forcing them to deploy early, slow down their advance and affect their morale.

AIR OPTIONS

PARACHUTE

The forward deployment of recce and special forces troops is a worldwide tactic. With the sniper being an integral part of the commander's ability to gather intelligence on the enemy and to slow him down or harass him when required, it makes sense to have the option of para dropping a sniper screen into place. Added to this the sniper's ability to seriously hinder an enemy's ability to move, work or to administer his forces, an air-drop of snipers buys time to get the main force ready for deployment in UN-type operations or on limited deployments. In tactical air landing operations,

HELICOPTERS

As snipers operate in small numbers, they can be deployed or extracted by any one of the world's numerous support helicopters. The undeniable skills of today's pilots coupled to the advances in the ability to fly in any weather or light conditions means that the sniper can easily be air-lifted to a forward mounting base or drop-off point to give the commander not only up-to-date information on the enemy deployments and strengths, but also the ability to engage and hinder the enemy, whether to slow his advance or to pin him down for engagement by a larger force.

WATERBORNE OPTIONS

CANOES

The standard military canoe is a two-man craft and, as snipers most commonly deploy in two-man teams, the two would seem a perfect match. While it would be impractical to expect every unit to have access to canoes, for the units that do, this has to be a viable option, whether they are used on inland waterways or for infiltration from the sea.

RIGID RAIDERS/ASSAULT CRAFT

In some situations it is a viable option to deploy high speed assault boats. Although noisy, this can be an ideal way to covertly drop off a sniper pair under the cover of a more vis-

ible operation involving larger numbers of troops. This tactic is effective as it is possible to put a small craft in to the shoreline or river bank in such a way as to conceal the exact number of troops that deploy from it, whether at night or in broad daylight. This means that even if the landing was observed the enemy has no way of knowing if anyone is left in the area when he observes the extraction, once the team has been ashore long enough for the snipers to disappear.

SUBMARINES

Although this limited to very few units, it is still an option. If the infiltration is from the sea, one of the best ways to covertly deploy troops ashore has to be from a submarine, whether it is an ocean-going craft or a mini-sub.

SPECIAL FORCES

This covers only a few of the options in which snipers can be deployed. While some of the choices are never going to be made available to the average infantry sniper and are more the province of special forces, the sniper needs to be aware of all the options. Who knows when a sniper force may have to deploy to defend against special forces infiltration? To know the enemy's options improves a sniper's ability to out-think and out-plan them.

The sniper should also remember that sniping is not a special forces' skill. It is an infantry skill, but the special forces do have snipers and will deploy them, so the more the infantry sniper learns about them and the more open minded he is, the less likely it is that he will be caught out. The sniper should never dismiss a suggestion or option until he has given it fair consideration. What might at first seem comical may eventually become not only successful, but also a new tactic or SOP for snipers the world over. Careless disregard for advice or arrogance can cost lives.

ABOVE: Snipers fast-roping from an RAF Puma support helicopter, a quick and effective way to rapidly deploy sniper teams.

BELOW: The ultimate goal is the successful deployment of snipers to carry out their mission, and their subsequent safe recovery.

INDEX

A

Accuracy International 338 Super Magnum sniper rifle, 99, 104, 140
Accuracy International AW (All Weather) sniper rifle, 44, 46, 104
Accuracy International L96A1 sniper rifle, 104
Accuracy International sniper rifle, 19
Accuracy International Tactical Suppressed sniper rifle, 103
Aerial photography, 32, 49
Agincourt (archers at), 12
Aiming off (shooting moving targets), 101
All-terrain vehicles (ATVs), 122
Ambush method (shooting moving targets), 100
American Civil War, 12
American War of Independence, 10
Ammunition, 96
Arctic conditions, 77
Armoured vehicles, 130
Armstrong, Major Neville, 13
Attitudes (toward snipers), 8

B

Baker rifles, 12
Balkans, 17, 129
Barrett M82A1 "Light Fifty" sniper rifle, 86, 111, 140
Beirut, 129
Belfast, Northern Ireland, 134
Berdan's Sharpshooters, 12
Binoculars, 31 et seq, 38
Binoculars, Camouflaging, 33, 73
Bipods, 101
Boer War (1899-1902), 13
Boots, 26, 35, 71
Bosnia, 17, 133
Boys' anti-tank rifle, 111
Breathing (while shooting), 94
British Army 1st SOS (School of Sniping), 13
British Army 95th Rifles (Royal Green Jackets), 12
British Army King's Rifle Corps, 12
British Royal Marines, 16, 21
British snipers, 18, 19, 20, 23, 24, 26, 31, 32, 33, 35, 38, 43, 45, 46, 50, 54, 60, 61, 65, 70, 73, 77, 78, 86, 87, 98, 99, 100, 112, 122, 126, 127, 129, 136
British snipers, World War I, 13 et seq

British snipers, World War II, 15
Browning handgun, 19
Bushes (as hides), 81

C

Camouflage and concealment, 60 et seq
Camouflage patterns, 66 et seq
Camouflage, German Army fleck tarn, 19
Camouflage, Natural, 75 et seq
Camouflage, Thermal, 84
Camouflage, Urban, 78
Center Mass, Inc., 101, 102
Chandler, Colonel Norman (USMC), 106
Chandler sniper rifle, 106
Chechnya, 17, 129
Clothing (effects on shooting), 97
Communications, 30, 42
Cooper, Malcolm, 104
Cover, Use of, 76
Croatia, 17

D

Daylight reconnaissance, 136, 137
Defensive operations, 115
DeLisle sentry-removing weapon, 109
Deployment of snipers, 112 et seq
Desert conditions, 76
Desert Patrol Vehicles (Land Rovers), 122
Desert Storm, Operation, 76
Distance, Judging, 35 et seq
Distance, Judging, training, 40
Dragunov SVD sniper rifle, 48, 108

E

EDICT (Elevation, Deflection, Indication, Confirmation and Time), 31

F

Face, Camouflaging the, 70, 71
Face masks, US tank drivers', 68
Feet, Camouflaging the, 71
Female snipers, 15
Finnish snipers, World War II, 15
Fire base positions, 123
Fire, Application of 96
Foliage (as camouflage), 75 et seq
French snipers, 33, 39, 46, 51, 58, 74, 99, 121, 124, 135

French special forces, 61, 91
FRF1/FRF2 sniper rifle, 59, 99, 109

G

Gaythorn-Hardy, 13
German sniper, 59, 100
German snipers, World War I, 13 et seq, 85
Ghillie suits, 60 et seq
Gloves, 69
Gray, Major George, 13
GRIT (Group, Range, Indication and Type), 31
Grouping (shots), 95
Gulf War, 17, 76, 122, 123
Gurkha snipers (British Army), 27, 29, 36, 41, 47, 54, 65, 74, 95, 106, 116

H

Hands, Camouflaging the, 69
Harassing the enemy, 115
Hathcock, Carlos, 17
Hawkins shooting position, 89
Hawkins (modified) shooting position, 90
Hayha (Finnish sniper), 15
Head, Camouflaging the, 68
Heckler & Koch MSG-90 sniper rifle, 107
Heckler & Koch PSG-1 rifle, 107
Helicopters, Disabling, 114
Hesketh-Pritchard, Major, 13, et seq
Hessian (camouflage material), 61 et seq
Hides, Construction and use of, 79 et seq
Hides, Urban, 82
Humidity (effects on shooting), 97

I

Infrared optics, 136
Internal security operations, 129, 130
IRA (Irish Republican Army), 108, 111
Ireland, Northern, 78, 79
Iron Brigade Armories Chandler sniper rifle, 106

J

Japanese snipers, World War II, 16
Jungle conditions, 77

K

Kalashnikov rifles, 108, 109
Kipling, Rudyard, 8
Kneeling shooting positions, 92
Kolkka (Finnish sniper), 15
Konings, Major (German sniper), 15 et seq
Kosovo, 17, 133

L

Laid back shooting position, 25, 90
Land Rover, 72, 113
Langford-Lloyd, 13
Laser range finders, 39
Lee-Enfield No4T sniper rifle, 19
Leica laser range finders, 31
Leica Vecta binoculars, 31
Light conditions, 26
Light vehicles, 122
Lovat, Lord, 60
Lovat Scouts, 60

M

M21 sniper rifle (US Army), 105
M24 sniper rifle, 116
M40A1/A2/A3 sniper rifle (USMC), 105
Map reading, 32, 49
Marksmanship principles, 86
MAS 36 rifle, 109
Mawhinney, Chuck, 17
McBride, Captain Herbert, 13
Mirage (effects on shooting), 97
Mogadishu, 129, 133
Motorcycles, 122
Moving targets, 100 et seq

N

Night observation, 27 et seq
Night vision aids/optics, 25, 135, 136
Noise suppression (of weapons), 103
Normandy, 16
North-West Wind, US Private, 15
Nuclear, biological and chemical conditions, 137

O

Observation points, 14
Observation training, 32
Obstacles, Sniper assistance at, 122
Offensive operations, 114
Optical aids, 24 et seq

Optics, 63, 97
Optics, Thermal, 85

P

Paine, Dr. Roger, 16
Parker-Hale M85 sniper rifle, 106, 107
Peninsular War (1808-1814), 12
Personal equipment, Camouflaging, 72
PGM Commando sniper rifle, 91, 110
PGM Hecate sniper rifle, 110
Photography, 48
Pistol, Combat, training, 46
Police marksmen, 17
Prone and lying shooting position, 88
Prone bipod shooting position, 88
Puma helicopter, 141

Q

Quad vehicle, 122, 140

R

Radio communications, Disabling, 114
Rain (effects on shooting), 97
Range card, 29
Range estimation, 40
Range finding, 35 et seq
Reconnaissance role, 47, 115
Relief operations, Sniper, 127
Remington 700 series rifle, 105
Rifles, Camouflaging, 74
Russian snipers, World War II, 15 et seq

S

SA80 assault rifle, 19
Saab laser firing attachment, 42
Saab laser training simulator, 113
Scimitar recce vehicle, 45
Screens, Sniper, 125
Search methods, 26 et seq
Serbia, 17
Sharps .52 calibre rifle, 12
Sharpshooting, 17
Shooting aids, 101
Shooting (grouping shots), 95
Shooting positions, 87 et seq
Shooting techniques, 86 et seq
Shooting, miss drill, 98
Shooting, Operational snap, 98
Shooting, Poor, checklist, 97
Shore, Captain (R.A.F. Regiment), 16

Sierra Leone, 77, 133, 134
SIMRAD night sight, 105
Sitting shooting positions, 91
Skin, Camouflaging the, 69
Slovenian snipers, 34, 48, 68
Sniper advance deployment, 121
  air insertion, 140
  ambush forces, 121
  ambush position, 115
  ambush training, 50
  APC insertion, 139
  attack roles, 123
  camouflage and concealment training, 49 et seq
  canoe insertion, 140
  close target reconnaissance, 47
  combat pistol training, 46
  communications, 30
  control, 117
  counter-surveillance, 120
  covert scouting patrols, 128
  cross-training (international), 18, 46
  defensive role, 125
  deployment, 19
  employment principles, 116 et seq
  endurance, 119
  escape and evasion training, 43
  fire base positions, 123
  foreign weapon training, 45
  forward air control, 45
  helicopter insertion, 140
  indirect fire control, 44
  insertion by foot, 138
  insertion methods, 121, et seq, 137 et seq
  instructors, 20, 21, 22, 31, 32, 42, 48 et seq
  knowledge, 41 et seq
  leopard crawl technique, 56
  main defensive position tasks, 127
  monkey run technique, 56
  motorcycle insertion, 139
  movement techniques, 58
  navigation training, 48
  NBC procedures, 43, 137
  night operations, 135 et seq
  observation skills, 23 et seq
  operations other than war, 133
  pair deployment, 117
  pair equipment, 72
  parachute insertion, 140
  patrolling, 128
  photography training, 48
  pistol training, 21, 22
  protection and back-up, 118
  quad and ATV insertion, 139
  qualities, 20 et seq

range card, 29
range-finding measures, 36
recognition training, 43
relief operations, 127
reorganisation role, 124
rigid raider/assault craft insertion, 140
rules of engagement, 119
screens, 125
selection, 20 et seq
shooting positions, 8, 9
shooting techniques, 86 et seq
shooting training, 86 et seq
skills, 21
stalking, 54 et seq
stomach crawl techniques, 56
submarine insertion, 141
survival training,, 43
tactical employment, 120
targets in the advance, 122
targets in the attacking force, 127
targets in the defensive position, 127
targets in the screen, 127
tasks in civilian areas, 135
tasks in the withdrawal, 132
tasks, 117
training, 19 et seq
urban covert entry, 131
urban hides, 131
urban role, 129
vision (daylight/night-time), 28
walk techniques, 56
waterborne insertion, 140
weapons, 104 et seq
withdrawal operations, 132
Sniper: British Army definition, 17, 21
Snipers and observers, 10
Snow, Camouflage in, 78
Special Air Service, British, 77, 122
Special forces, 18, 67, 103
Spotting scopes, 40
Stalingrad, 15 et seq
Standing shooting positions, 59, 93
Steyr SSG sniper rifle, 107

Suppressed weapon capability, 103
Surveillance devices, 120, 136
Surveillance and target acquisition plan (SNAP), 120

T
Tactical Sharpshooter Rifle Rest, 102
Tanks, Disabling, 113
Target estimation from height, 100
Target leads (shooting moving targets), 101
Target listing, 30
Target selection, 112 et seq
Targets (for sniper training), 95
Targets, Moving, 100
Telescopes, Camouflaging, 74
Telescopic sights, 53
Temperature (effects on shooting), 96
Terrorists, 130
TESEX, British simulation exercise, 19
Theatres of operation, 76 et seq
Thermal imaging, Defeating, 85
Thermal imaging, sights, 84
Thermal optics, 136
Tracking method (shooting moving targets), 100
Trees (as shooting platforms), 34
Trench periscopes, 14
Trigger control, 94
Tripods, 101
Tripods, Improvised, 37, 38

U
Underhill, Captain, 13
Urban camouflage, 79, 82
Urban conditions, 78
Urban role of the sniper, 129
Urban sniping, 94
Urban warfare, 129
US Army snipers, World War I, 14
US Marine Corps, 18, 129
US Marine Corps M40 sniper rifle, 105

US Marine Corps snipers, 17
US Marine Scout-Sniper School, 18
US Marine Training Battalion, 106

V
Vietnam War, 10, 17, 108
Vision, Sniper's, 28
VSS silent sniper rifle, 109

W
Warrior IFV, 140
Weapon adjustment, 97
Weapon camouflage, 70
Weapon destruction drills, 103
Weapon handling, 87
Weapon rests, 101
Weapons and equipment (British, current), 19
Weapons and equipment (British, World War II), 19
Weapons, Camouflaging, 72
Weapons, Current operational sniper, 104 et seq
Weapons, Foreign, 45
Weapons, Heavy, Disabling, 114
Wind (effects on shooting), 98
Wind strength, direction and values, 99, 100
World War I, 9, 13, 23, 60
World War I sniper defensive devices, 14
World War I sniper suits (British), 13
World War II, 8, 15 et seq, 18, 77, 85
World War II British Army sniper-training manual, 16
World War II German camouflage uniforms, 15
World War II German sniper rifle suppressor, 16

Z
Zaitsev, Vassili (Russian sniper), 15 et seq